DF

2012

D0403652

POT PSYCHOLOGY'S
HOW to BE

POT PSYCHOLOGY'S
HOW to BE
Lowbrow Advice
from High People

Tracie Egan Morrissey
and Rich Juzwiak
Illustrations by Lindsay Mound

GRAND CENTRAL
PUBLISHING

NEW YORK   BOSTON

Grand Central Publishing
Hachette Book Group
237 Park Avenue
New York, NY 10017

www.HachetteBookGroup.com

Printed in the United States of America

RRDC

First Edition: November 2012
10 9 8 7 6 5 4 3 2 1

Grand Central Publishing is a division of Hachette Book Group, Inc.
The Grand Central Publishing name and logo is a trademark of Hachette Book Group, Inc.

The Hachette Speakers Bureau provides a wide range of authors for speaking events. To find out more, go to www.hachettespeakersbureau.com or call (866) 376-6591.

The publisher is not responsible for websites (or their content) that are not owned by the publisher.

Library of Congress Cataloging-in-Publication Data
Morrissey, Tracie Egan.
    Pot psychology's how to be: low-minded advice from high people / by Tracie Egan Morrissey and Rich Juzwiak; illustrations by Lindsay Mound.
        p. cm.
    ISBN 978-1-4555-0281-3 (pbk.)
    1. Marijuana—Humor.   2. Conduct of life—Humor.   3.   Etiquette—Humor.
I. Juzwiak, Richard.   II. Title.
    PN6231.M24M67 2012
    818'.602—dc23
                                                              2012014072

To Anna Nicole Smith: You lit up our lives, but not our bong. We miss you every day.

And to Judge Judith Sheindlin: You remain our moral compass, even though we know you wouldn't approve.

Finally, if we may, we would love to dedicate this book to all the parents and children of the world.

Contents

Sex and Love Non-Problems   85

Body and Diet Non-Problems   195

Self-Improvement Non-Problems   233

Intro

Nobody needs advice, but everybody *wants* it. Conversely, everybody wants to give advice, but we *need* to. It's in our blood...because we're stoned. That's the point. And what better way to legitimize two stoned people's need to babble advice than with a book?

By nature of the deal we have been given to write this book, we are professionals. But don't get it twisted: we are not experts.

Allow us to introduce ourselves: we're Tracie and Rich. We go way back. We met as teenagers in 1998, during our freshman year at NYU. We were at a dorm party where lesbians and gay men were making out with each other. Tracie had short hair and glasses; Rich approached her and asked, "Do you like Ani DiFranco?" That was not a come-on. Rich is gay. We didn't kiss (and Tracie is not a lesbian, anyway), but we did shotgun a joint. From there, a friendship was born.

Flash-forward fourteen years. We host an Internet video series in which we answer viewer-submitted questions, solving their problems with the help of an herbal remedy. Basically we get stoned and tell people how to live their lives. We give our two cents (or 420 sense?) on all of life's non-problems from party etiquette, problems in the workplace, what religion to be, to whether or not your boyfriend/girlfriend/parent/friend/teacher/pet is gay. We say "non-problems" because we're not trying to cure cancer here (you may notice that this book is not called *How to Cure Cancer*). We're just trying to be the joint that makes the chemo more bearable.

We consider this a reference book for people who are too stoned to think for themselves. Catering to stoners' attention span—by which we mean the lack thereof—we present 101 of life's non-problems solved as quickly as we see fit and as briefly as we wanna be. This is intended to be a guide for people to carry through life. Because you never know when life will present a non-problem outside of a WiFi hot zone. (And that's a non-problem solved right there.)

We're confident in our ability to tell people how to be. Because we know how to be us. We're not saying we're the best. We're just saying we're better.*

Anyway, we have advice, whether you want it or not. We're mostly joking and half serious so take us with a grain of salt...N-Pepa. Lookit, no matter how bad you think your situation is, if you have enough money to buy this book and some weed, life could be far worse. If you have a friend that you're borrowing this book from, why not hit him up for some money or other help if that's what you need? You're *his* problem, not ours.

Perhaps you are on the fence as to whether or not this book is for you. Below, you will read a list of all of our target demographics, so that you can decide if our advice applies. We foresee this book appealing to:

People who appreciate people who smoke weed
People who are confused
People who don't know what they want, but know that they want
    it briefly
People who are literate but don't normally read
Animals who can read
College kids
High Times readers
Showtime subscribers
Homosexuals
Closeted homosexuals

Ladies who munch

Chong (Cheech is a sellout)

Dr. Dre fans

Dr. Drew fans

Captive audiences (you know, prisoners, people in airports, people at the DMV, etc., as they're the people who usually are experiencing issues they might need help with, anyway)

Open-minded evangelicals

Your tired

Your poor

Your huddled masses yearning to breathe weed smoke

*Disclaimer: We're not responsible if you follow our advice on anything. And you should know that anyway, since we've already told you we're stoned. So you know, decide what kind of person you want to be: the kind who takes high people seriously, or the kind who doesn't. Don't let our feelings influence your decision here. But in the rest of the book you should. But it's not our fault if you do. Just sayin'.

Hypocritical Oath

We swear to fulfill, to the best of our ability and judgment,* this covenant:

We will respect the hard-won scientific gains of those physicians in whose steps we're too high to bother putting our shoes on to walk in, and gladly share our knowledge with all y'all.

We will apply, for the benefit of the sickos out there, all measures that are required (or at least that we can perform, which is none), avoiding therapeutic nihilism but engaging in overtreatment as much as possible because we have a word count to hit.

We will remember that there is art to advice giving as well as science, and that warmth, sympathy, understanding, cursing humorously, looking at animal pictures, fart discourse, sexy talk, and Judge Judy worship may outweigh the surgeon's knife, but never the chemist's drug.

We will not be ashamed to say, "We know not," because we don't. When the skills of another are needed for a reader's recovery, we will probably fail to call in our colleagues because we won't find their numbers.

We won't respect the privacy of our patients, sorry. We're horrible at keeping secrets, and if you disclose to us your problem, it is primarily so the world may know. Most especially we must tread with care in matters of life and death, because those are serious. Except, we might even giggle about those as well. Sorry, we're high and we're doing our best. If it is given to us to save a life, all thanks. And by that, we mean, you better thank us. All thanks for us, thanks. It is not within our power to take a life, unless you slit your wrists with a page of this book. If not, relax and stop taking things so seriously. This awesome responsibility of book writing must be faced with great humility and awareness of our own frailty, which we probably will not let on. Above all, we must not play at God. But we can play with ourselves, as this is our playpen.

We will remember that we do not treat a boner, an overgrown pubic area, or a musical queef, but rather a misguided human being whose problem may affect his or her family and economic prospects. Our responsibility doesn't extend to those related problems, if we are to care adequately for the troubled. One thing at a time, people.

We will prevent disease whenever we can by wearing condoms, except for when it feels better without them (i.e., always). Prevention is preferable to a cure, just like not wearing condoms is preferable to wearing condoms. Ponder that contradiction.

We will remember that we remain members of society, with special obligations to all our fellow human beings or the ones who bought this book, anyhow: the five of you that are sound of mind and body as well as the infirm.

If we do not violate this oath, it will be a miracle, especially because we barely know what it says. May we enjoy life and art (stoned), be respected while we live (stoned), and be remembered with affection thereafter (by people whose memories still work after being stoned). May we always act so as to preserve the finest traditions of our call-ing by our publisher and may we long experience the joy of healing those who are lost and misguided enough to seek our help. Forever and ever, amen.

---

*Our judgment and ability are questionable, and for that reason we reserve the right to revoke any of our claims, give contradictory advice, go back on our word, be completely arbitrary, forget what we said, and otherwise spout whatever shit comes into our heads.

A Note on the Party Animals

As you page through this book, you may think that we're into animals. You'd be right. We are into animals, but not like *that*. We're very open-minded about almost everything because we don't care about most things, but bestiality and incest are two practices that we're resolutely against. Even when we're at our most arbitrary and forgetful of our own stance, we remain anti-bestiality and anti-incest. There's no joke to tell there: it's just how it is.

In this book, each "non-problem page," as we've come to call them, is illustrated with a picture of a pet, somehow invoking the theme of the non-problem. We call these the Party Animals. We love anthropomorphized animals (especially Rich, whose mom is a talking-dog movie enthusiast, so he basically has anthropomorphized animals in his blood). And also, just in case you don't have an eye for subtlety, we're drawing the parallel between people and animals because people *are* animals.

Please treat our Party Animals with the same love and respect as you would your own pets. But please don't masturbate to images of them, because then we'll have to kill you.

Etiquette Non-Problems

How to Be Stoned in Public

It always seems like a good idea to get stoned before leaving the house, but it rarely ever is. For this reason, our first piece of advice is: don't get stoned before leaving the house. But we'd be hypocrites if we truly expected you to live by those words.

If you're planning on leaving the house stoned, make like a Boy Scout and be prepared (but don't make like a Boy Scout and be anti-gay). Eyedrops are essential, but use them sparingly in public, as the only thing that's more of a giveaway than bloodshot, glassy eyes is a giggling fool with a bottle of Visine. Think of every trip out of the house as an expedition, and pack fluids and trail mix or some kind of dehydrated food accordingly. (We recommend freeze-dried ice cream even though it is like an unholy mixture of chalk and circus peanuts. It will, at least, give you something to think about. How do you make freeze-dried ice cream? What is freeze-drying? That's something to ponder, and everyone should be so lucky as to have something to ponder on their person.) Don't even think about your outfit. Just go. Changing your outfit before you leave could put you in a spiral of indecision and second-guessing. You may never get out the door. Say good-bye to your pets, but do not turn it into a belabored farewell. They don't care, and you're talking to animals. Just because you're stoned doesn't mean the rest of the world is. Remember to shut the door behind you, but before you do, remember to grab your keys. That may sound obvious, but such reminders are necessary when you're stoned.

Here's another: don't forget to think. People smoke pot to take their mind off of things, but the irony is that your mind must now be on everything. Don't assume that anything will work out automatically. It won't. Isn't that the point of leaving the safe haven of your home while stoned, after all? By choosing to do so, you are challenging your challenged brain. The simplest tasks, such as making small talk with a neighbor in your hallway, will seem harder, and more advanced social interactions, like running into an ex on the street, will seem impossible. In the case of the neighbor in the hallway, don't try to pretend that you're sober—she can smell the air outside your door. A polite giggle or scowl, depending on your preexisting relationship, is sufficient. In the case of your ex on the street, cross to the other side as soon as it's safe. You may want to ask a stranger if it's safe, because you're probably in no position to judge safety. What are you, some kind of inspector? Never mind, we don't think you should talk to strangers. Why are you wasting all this time? It's getting really awkward with your ex in the immediate vicinity. No matter where you are, throw caution to the wind and cross the street right now! Go!

If you've made it this far and are still alive, or at least able to read, know that you can cross only so many streets. You're going to have to deal with people in public. Understand that no matter how weird you feel, you are not alone. Everybody feels weird. You just happen to be hyperaware of it. Don't cower by doing things like avoiding eye contact. Everybody can see you and your stony eyes whether you are looking at them or not. (Unless you are wearing sunglasses, which is also a great idea for helping to prevent crow's-feet. However, don't wear sunglasses at night. You are not Corey Hart.)

The best thing to do is embrace your eccentricity, which in this case probably has mostly to do with you being stoned. Don't suppress your laughter—it will only make it worse, and thus harder to suppress. Weed has a way of turning suppressed laughter into snorting. Plus, didn't you get stoned in the first place to laugh more? Everything is funnier when you're high, except for internal conflict. Stop fighting your urges. Any exchange that you have will feel more awkward than it is, though it probably would have been awkward in the first place, unless you're the weird type to make friends with your local convenience-store worker. In that case, the weed is the least of your problems.

Basically, just be calm. Give yourself time, stop and smell the roses, and think about how weird the word *roses* is. Roses. Roses. Roses. Say it out loud. Again. When you say it enough times, it stops being a word and becomes a sentence. Rose is. But what is she exactly?

Feel better?

How to Be Openly Gay

1. Use words:

Go up to people (but not animals, because they don't under-stand English) and tell them you're gay. But if you're an animal, and you're reading this, you can tell people you're gay by having sex in front of them.

2. Use actions:

As we told the animals, have sex in front of people. They'll figure it out. There are other ways to be gay, but this one hits the nail on the head.

How to Be a Parent
Who Isn't a Hypocrite About
Your Kid Smoking Pot

This is a hot-button/hot-boxing topic primarily as a result of that '80s PSA, in which a chronically interruptive father confronts his drummer son with a cigar box full of recreational drugs belonging to him. The son responds with the immortal words that made no sense to most of the kids who were young enough to be paying attention and not making out or doing drugs of their own during commercial breaks: "*You*, all right? I learned it by watching *you*." No one wants their kid to grow up to be a loser drummer druggie, and everyone wants to continue doing the drugs they did before the kids came along, harshed their parents' mellow, and pooped their party. How do you strike the balance?

You cannot. You are a hypocrite, but at least you're a high hypocrite. Your sticks of pot must be consumed when your children are asleep, out of town, or freshly dead in their beds. Get used to braving the winter and elements in exchange for a buzz. The days of zoning out are behind you, which means your general paranoia will now be accompanied by paranoia regarding your children's well-being and their lives that you are probably fucking up, both with and without the help of marijuana.

If you happen to catch your kid smoking pot, you may not have failed as a parent, but as a secret-keeper. The weirdo pedo voice that comes on at the end of that PSA and intones, "Parents who use drugs have children who use drugs," says it for a reason. We could provide you statistics, but you're stoned and you wouldn't understand them anyway. If you're so interested in numbers, buy a calculator. And let's face it: if you were so interested in raising your children to be drug free, you wouldn't have brought this book into your home. Luckily for you, we have pictures of animals.

...Or maybe that's unlucky because it makes this book so much more appealing to children and stoners alike. Or maybe children stoners. Maybe all of the world's children become your children when you write a book. Maybe *we're* the bad parents, and this entry is our struggle with our own hypocrisy put into words. If that's the case, we can live with it. We never (at least, not yet in this book) said we weren't hypocrites or bad influences, which makes us actually not very hypocritical at all. So, the answer of how not to be a hypocrite in the case of children and marijuana is the same answer as how not to be a hypocrite, period: don't say you aren't a hypocrite. Give people the lowest expectations possible. A good way to do this is to be visibly stoned. No one's going to expect a lot out of a person, parent, or pet with bloodshot eyes, a fit of the giggles, a case of the munchies, and a feed bag of snack mix. This counsel may result in terrible parenting, but that's not a problem we intend to solve in this book. We'll leave that to the children because, after all, we believe the children are our future.

How to Be Around Whores

You know who hung out with whores all the time? Jesus. Even though we're supposed to believe he was born of a virgin and never married or had sex before he died when he was thirty-three, it's pretty well documented that Jesus loved his prostitutes. He stood up for them when they were being picked on. He never made them feel like they were beneath him (even if they literally were—free of charge, of course). He hung out with hookers. He traveled with hookers. He partied with hookers. He knew they were fun. Above all, he didn't judge them.

Anytime you are around whores and don't know how to behave, just ask yourself, *What would Jesus do?* The answer is: don't cast stones at hookers; get stoned with hookers.

Hookers are people, too, so speak to them like people. Here is a list of suggested topics:

- Hairspray
- Heels
- Herpes
- Menstruation (Note: if you are with a hooker at the Point, as seen on the classic HBO documentary series *Hookers at the Point*, you may get further by pronouncing this "menestration.")
- The influence of Samantha Fox on their lives
- The influence of *Pretty Woman* on their lives
- Pimps
- Suitcase pimps
- Pornography: possible career direction?
- Stripping: is she through with it, or aspiring to it?
- Price points
- Exploitation: who's zoomin' who—the ho or the john?
- Streetwalking pros and cons
- Streetwear
- What songs she sings to pass the time while at work
- Panties: necessary or necessary evil?

- Perks
- Vacation time
- Cocaine
- Weird tricks
- Weird vagina tricks
- Penis size
- Condom taste
- Clientele: lesbians?
- Day care providers
- Night care providers
- Politics
- Literature
- Viral videos
- Viral outbreaks
- Whether appearing in a documentary on prostitution is an aspiration
- Whores/hookers/hoes/prostitutes—What does she prefer to be called? What is the semantic hierarchy?
- Past molestation
- Past masturbation
- Orgasms: are they even possible in this scenario?
- How has the Internet changed the industry?

And, since this question can be interpreted in multiple ways, here are some suggestions of how to be in the proximity of whores:

- Go to Atlantic City
- Go to the Moonlite Bunny Ranch
- Go to a street corner (any one will do—a hooker's bound to walk by at some point)
- Go on Craigslist (but not if you are a murderer, because "Craigslist killer" is such a cliché nowadays)
- Go to any major metropolitan area

- Go to a club
- Go to the champagne room
- Go under the boardwalk
- Go to a hardware store
- Go to Rodeo Drive (those salesgirls are bigger whores than streetwalkers, or so say Romy and Michelle)

How to Be Around
Religious Weirdos

If you can't beat 'em, read their scriptures. A bit of distance turns holy into hilarious, so the entertainment value could be high. Take, for example, the Book of Mormon, which is full of historical inaccuracies and racism (the Lamanites—aka the bad guys—are characterized as "dark, filthy, and loathsome"). Read it and be amazed. Actually, we can't say that for sure, because we haven't read it, but we have read books that quote it. And that is enough to converse with Mormons (also something we haven't done).

At the very least, take the opportunity to have a cultural experience and learn about the ways of people with whom you have little in common, thank God (if you believe in him). Make like a Christian and be nice to their faces and laugh at them behind their backs. But do not let genuine curiosity and your sense of humor open the door for cults. They're scary and they'll suck you right in. Professionals* agree: cults'll getcha.

If you find that interacting with a religious weirdo leads to an argument, make sure you are not outside of an abortion clinic, because the weirdo might be armed. It's all fun and games until you bring artillery into things. Then, it's life or death, and that's a little too hardcore for something that you're doing just to laugh about later. If your religious weirdo seems not of the dangerous variety but is still confrontational or adamant about inundating you with their beliefs (or worse yet: literature—who wants to carry around all that paper?), the most important thing is to remain calm. They're the weirdos—so let them be the freaks. They will dig their own graves for the sake of getting into heaven.

For your points, stick to logic. You seem like a straight shooter invested in rational thinking, so do what you were put on this Earth (by God?) to do. You will find that their arguments generally boil down to: "Because the Bible tells me so." Understand that what you're dealing with is someone who talks to books. That is all the justification you need for your case. You win—all you have to do is let them lose.

But this is really a worst-case scenario. Religion actually helps a lot of people be nice, or at least do a good job of pretending to be. So, that's at least pleasant. Maybe the best way to go about things is to avoid any serious talk and observe them in as detached a way as possible. No matter what they say nod politely and smile while taking mental notes for that novel you're working on. Let them do your job.

*Us.

How to Be a Bitch Without Being a Female Dog

Bitch is a hot-button word, and even though it often refers to females, when we say "hot-button," we do not mean clitoral. When applied to a human female, bitch can have several different meanings. It's kind of like *Aloha*, the Hawaiian word for everything. A compliment and a curse alike, its connotation comes down to intention. Do you own *bitch* or does someone own you by calling you one? Are you the bitch of *bitch*? Or is *bitch* your bitch? Or, most ideally, are you a female dog who can read?

Here we will help you be the best bitch you can be by giving you pointers on how to be a good bitch versus a bad bitch. It's kind of like *The Wizard of Oz* with PMDD (that's premenstrual dysphoric disorder... and if you think PMS is bad, well, she's worse than the other one was!).

Do: Roll your eyes when someone tells you to smile.
Don't: Lick your vagina just because you can. At least, not in public.

Do: Give someone the finger when they cut you off on the highway.
Don't: Slam into their car with yours, killing someone in the process.

Do: Speak out against sexism whenever you see it.
Don't: Bark about sexism.

Do: File your nails when someone's talking to you.
Don't: File them into points and then stab that person in the neck.

Do: Reject an unfit suitor's advances.
Don't: Hump his leg.

Do: Uncross and recross your legs to drive a point home.
Don't: Wear panties when you do this.

Do: Eat the last French fry of a shared order.
Don't: Lick it and put it back on the plate.

Do: Flip your hair.
Don't: Plant it in someone's food.

Do: Snap your gum.
Don't: Snap bras.

Do: Give attitude to TSA agents who are groping you.
Don't: Give rabies to TSA agents who are groping you.

Do: Audibly gag whenever the situation calls for it.
Don't: Throw up and eat it.

Do: Laugh when someone trips.
Don't: Laugh if they die.

Do: Show up your fellow diners by bringing an expensive bottle of wine to a dinner party.
Don't: Leave with it if it hasn't been opened.

Do: Keep your man/partner/roommate on a short leash.
Don't: Let them do the same.

Do: Yell back at catcalling construction workers.
Don't: Pee on their scaffolding.

Do: Grab the last bathing suit in your size off the rack if you see someone else eyeing it.
Don't: Try it on without underwear and put it back on the rack.

Do: Speak openly about your period wherever you damn well please.
Don't: Empty your keeper (or any other reusable device you're using to collect your menstrual blood) in the sink in a public bathroom, especially if there are other people around.

Do: Whatever you need to do to catch a cab during rush hour.
Don't: Chase after cabs for the hell of it.

Do: Feel free to talk shit behind someone's back.
Don't: Say it to his or her face (unless you're on reality TV).

Do: Eat as many biscuits as you want.
Don't: Eat dog biscuits.

Do: Use sex toys whenever you have sex, especially if your partner says it makes him or her feel inadequate.
Don't: Use chew toys whenever you have sex.

Do: Butt in front of other people when buying a drink at the bar.
Don't: Sniff other people's butts (in public).

How to Be a Bitch
at a Bitch's Wedding

If you are not on good standing with a person who's getting married but for some reason are still going to her wedding, there are going to be so many people around that your best bet is to let your bitch flag fly not with words or even actions, but with fashion. Any outfit calculated to take attention away from the bride is an outfit worth wearing. We recommend wearing sequins to steal some of her shine, or wearing white to show everyone else how it's really done. Other fashion choices to consider:

- Spandex
- Lamé, gold or otherwise
- Halloween costumes (the sluttier the better)
- Novelty wigs
- Obvious lace front wigs or extensions
- Falls and/or Bumpits that make your hair so high that no one sitting behind you in church can see the altar
- Tap shoes
- A cape
- A visible garter belt
- A tutu
- Bunny ears
- Anything Helena Bonham Carter would wear, because then you're obviously just trying to be an asshole
- Mismatched shoes
- Sneakers
- No bra
- Pasties
- Jingle bells
- Fingerless gloves
- Leather pants
- A leather harness
- A strap-on

- Face paint
- Roller skates
- Wax lips
- Shin guards
- Raver pants
- Parachute pants
- Buttless pants
- Lace everywhere
- A tiara
- A veil
- A wedding dress

How to Be Courteous
to the Disabled

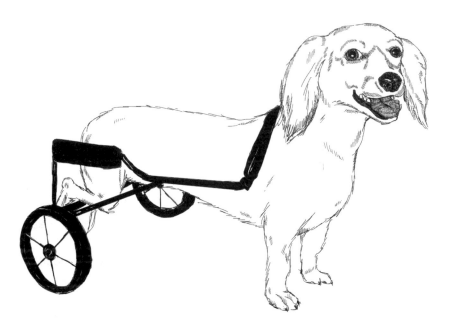

(Note: This section is written assuming that you aren't disabled. If you are, you probably already know this information, or you need to backtrack and get a lesson in basic empathy. We cannot help you there. Find your own crutch.)

In all bathrooms, your judgment is of utmost importance, but once you introduce handicapped stalls into the picture, shit gets serious. First and foremost, we understand that handicapped bathrooms are luxurious compared to other stalls. If you don't understand this, try going to your junior prom and giving birth in a regular stall and then going to your senior prom and giving birth in a handicapped one. Anyway, handicapped stalls are for the disabled, not for you, unless you want us to make you disabled. We're serious about this. We don't like that shit. Make handicapped stalls your last choice unless the bathroom is so crowded that your principles slow everyone else down, effectively making them disabled.

Now let's talk about handicapped parking spots. Unlike handicapped stalls, you can actually get a ticket for using these when you don't need them. So even just on a selfish level, it behooves you to keep your ass and your car's ass out of them.

But both of these are passive ways of treating disabled people. What happens when you come face-to-face or face-to-wheelchair with one of them? What should happen is that you become nicer than usual. Why make anyone's visibly-more-difficult life worse? Don't avoid eye contact with the disabled—in fact, engage in it. Avoiding eye contact will only make that person feel either invisible or freakish. So look, but just briefly: use as long as you need to take in and assess their situation, but don't linger beyond that. Because then you'll be staring and make them feel bad about that.

A good rule of thumb is to do everything you can to make a disabled person's life easier and nicer, even if that means going above and beyond what you'd do for a nondisabled person. If you haven't been to Disney World recently, you may not have had this important epiphany, but at Disney World disabled people are given priority. They get to cut even the Fast Pass line and go right to the front every time. This may irritate some who wait ninety minutes for a two-and-a-half-minute roller coaster ride in the dark, but chill out. A day at Disney World is a Day of the Disabled. It's their time to be better than everyone, and they seriously get, like, one of those days per year. (Unless they live in Anaheim, Orlando, Tokyo, or Marne-la-Vallée.) It is their time to shine brighter than the spokes of their wheelchairs (if that is the type of disabled person we're talking about). You're probably having an awesome day anyway, so mind your own beeswax, especially since it's perfectly able beeswax.

How to Be a Good Roommate
(Without Being a Doormat)

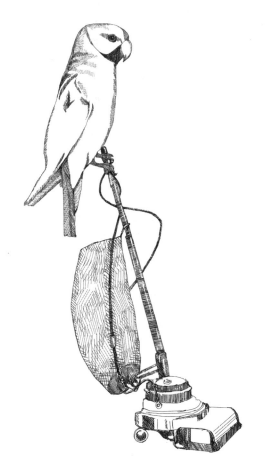

The key to being a good roommate is striking that perfect balance between being a ball-busting nag and a pushover. (This is actually the key to any effective communication.) You have to make like a skyscraper and give with resistance, while at the same time asserting yourself like a giant concrete-and-steel phallus. You can go back and forth and engage in power plays all day at work or at the Blooming-dale's cosmetics counter, but those are relatively easy to deal with because at the end of the day,* you can leave them all behind and retreat home. It's a particularly hairy situation, though, when you have to deal with these kinds of politics in the place that you live.

What do you do when you're confronted with the same kind of bullshit at home from someone you aren't even sleeping with? (And if you are, in fact, sleeping with him or her, you have even more problems than we are prepared to take on—slow down, take your roommate's penis and/ or vagina out of your mouth, and attack life, one page of this book at a time.) You can't harp on everything that doesn't swing the way you'd have it swing; *instead*, you must account for people's lifestyles, *since* not everybody was raised alike. You can't get on your roommate for leaving a pile of dishes in the sink for a day or two. Maybe he or she has just been super busy, and you should be accommodating about that kind of stress. At the same time, if it's been going on for two weeks or if accommodating the messiness of your roommate means accommodating a whole host of other roommates in the form of vermin, you have a concrete reason to voice protest. Where you can draw the line between justification and just being a dick is how concrete the problem is. If you're speaking out on principle, you're choosing your battles unwisely and potentially alienating someone who is not an alien by virtue of the fact that he or she lives in the same damn space as you. Your roommate has a large amount of power over your belongings because he or she has a key to your home. Don't forget that your personal property is constantly exposed to this person, and that you can't be home all hours of the day to look after it.

Even if you're doing it politely and are completely justified, asserting yourself can be a difficult thing, particularly when you're young. We've both been in situations where a simple, "Hey, don't do that!" would have been an easy thing to say and more or less solved the problem, but for whatever reason wrapped up in youth and a joint, we could not go there. So here's some of the more ridiculous shit we put up with from various roommates:

One roommate used Tracie's fabric scissors to trim his pubic hair and didn't even try to cover his tracks. In fact, he left his pubic hair not only all over the scissors, but all over the bathroom as well.

How we handled it: Screaming at him.

How we should have handled it: Stabbing him (with the pube-covered scissors, to give him back his hair).

One roommate was an aspiring bodybuilder who ate nothing besides chicken breasts and oats. He'd buy the old-fashioned big cardboard cylinder of Quaker Oats and scoop them into a bowl so carelessly that a few more oats would scatter around the kitchenette every time he ate them, which was every day. By the end of the semester, there was a layer of oats covering the entire floor.

How we handled it: By complaining behind his back and maybe saying once or twice, "Are you going to clean?"

How we should have handled it: By pointing out that the several invading vermin were direct results of the oats he'd left. We also could have laid down some hay to keep the obvious horse motif going.

One roommate shit with the door open. A lot.

How we handled it: By saying, "That smells not just like shit, but also like throw-up."

How we should have handled it: By shutting the door.

*   *   *

One roommate, upon moving to New York City, struck up a romantic relationship with a wrong number from Boston. She literally answered a misdirected call from him and then invited him to "sleep over" for a period of time that turned into six weeks. This was, by the way, in an apartment that could be described as a "studio" in only the most euphemistic way—it was actually a small cinder-block dorm room that was already being shared by two people. It was not unlike a prison cell.

How we handled it: Silence.

How we should have handled it: Screaming.

One roommate had day sex with a much older man (she was in college, he had white hair) when Tracie was home. This was in the other bedroom of a two-room "suite," except that bedroom didn't have a door or wall separating it from the common area because it was essentially the living room of an apartment that was supposed to be a one-bedroom. Instead of being embarrassed about this, the roommate bragged to Tracie later that she had lied to the white-haired man, telling him that she was a virgin.

How we handled it: Polite laughter masking actual laughter.

How we should have handled it: Vomiting. In her face.

One roommate had cybersex on Tracie's laptop and left all of the pictures traded during the experience on her desktop. She seriously doubts he even wiped off his hand when he quit out of the Internet browser.

How we handled it: By not saying anything. It was sexual and embarrassing.

How we should have handled it: By creating desktop wallpaper saying, "I know what you do when I'm not home."

*　　*　　*

One roommate left a very heavily used menstrual pad attached to a pair of panties in a common area. Tracie saw them and panicked, thinking they were hers. When she picked them up, she realized they weren't. She didn't even have to look at them closely, she knew as she lifted them, when the smell hit her nose. It was not her period smell. Tracie didn't even know that people had their own period smells until that moment.

How we handled it: Throwing them on the roommate's bed.

How we should have handled it: We did the right thing. It saved everyone embarrassment, and perhaps punished her by introducing her own stench to her own bed.

One roommate ate an entire batch of Rice Krispies Treats that Tracie had just made. At some point in his binge, he broke the casserole dish they were in and threw out the pieces. When Tracie woke in the morning, not only were there no Rice Krispies Treats, there was no sign of the dish...at first. On closer inspection, there was glass everywhere, but mostly under the refrigerator, where he had attempted to stash what was now hazardously sharp waste.

How we handled it: We asked him about it and were lied to in return. ("I have no idea what happened. I had no idea you made Rice Krispies Treats. I never saw a casserole dish.")

How we should have handled it: By boxing up the evidence and leaving it outside his door with an anonymous note saying: "I know what you did last night."

One roommate had the habit of removing lightbulbs from Tracie's lamps when his own would burn out. He wouldn't even bother to be sneaky and place his dead lightbulb in Tracie's lamp. In fact, he would leave his dead lightbulb by his lamp that now housed Tracie's more or less fresh lightbulb, essentially laying out the entire narrative.

How we handled it: By buying new lightbulbs.

How we should have handled it: Stuffing new and old lightbulbs up his ass.

*Literally, this time!

How to Be a Good Tipper

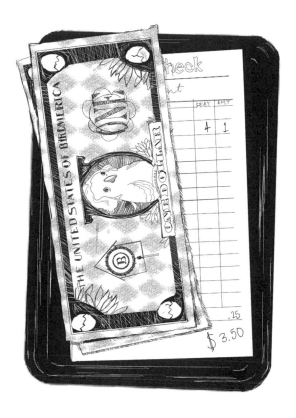

Leave 15 percent for adequate service, 20 percent if it's great, more if you're wealthy/famous and are angling for a mention in Page Six. What planet and/or country are you from that you don't know this? In fact, if you are from another country and you're here, learn our customs and tip accordingly. Unfortunately, in the U.S., a lot of people don't take kindly to foreigners, and their tipping style is doing them no favors.

How to Be at the Movies

A good rule of thumb is to behave in the movies as you would in church. "But guys, different churches require different decorum," you just said to us (we heard you). Exactly our point. Think of big-budget tent-pole comedies and horror movies as Pentecostal services: your participation is encouraged. Conversely, Oscar-bating dramas and confusing fare are more like a Catholic mass (psychological thrillers also fall into this category—emphasis on the psychological). Quirky indies are Unitarian, gentler comedies are Episcopalian, and musicals are Gay Church, duuuhh!

(We mean no offense to non-Christians by leaving you out. Seriously, we're doing a nice thing by not mocking your customs.)

Just like church, the movies are no place for a screaming baby. But unlike church, there will not be a cry room to retreat to, which means either get a sitter or leave the minute your kid opens his fucking trap. If you are a good parent, you will be compensated for all the scenes you missed when your children bring you DVDs to watch in the nursing home.

In church, the snacks are free, although meager. Even worse, communion wafers and cheap wine will likely give you bad breath. Unless you're a subscriber to the abstinence malarkey inevitably being preached by the church that gave you bad breath, you've got a problem. Anyway, did you know that snacks sold at the movies are packaged for minimum noise output? Basically, you are paying hand over fist for other people's comfort, and if you are a clod (and, let's face it, as an American, you are) that is the way it should be. As with church, sneaking snacks in is frowned upon, but you know you're going to do it anyway. Despite our respect for snack boxes with silencers, we also condone smuggling because we were both raised Catholic and are hypocrites.

And could you cool it with the texting? Those screens are very loud, visually. If you must text (or, in Rich's case, take notes for blog reviews), please do it on an iPhone, whose screen can be dimmed. As Rich* knows from note-taking experience, BlackBerries don't dim quite as well.

---

*Tracie is a normal person who doesn't take notes when she goes to the movies.

How to Be Polite About
Someone Else's Booger

Honestly, the polite thing to do is be like, "You have a booger." Because it's so much worse to let the person go through life and let this (possibly green) source of ridicule hang from his or her face while other people judge him or her for it. If you're uncomfortable with the word *booger*, who the hell are you? However, if this is the case, be vague. Rub your own nose and gesture toward his or hers. Encourage a bathroom or mirror visit. But whatever you do, give this person the tools to change the course of his or her day. Because wouldn't you want the same courtesy? An eye for an eye, a booger for a booger, an eye booger for an eye booger.

How to Be Polite About Someone Else's Spit

Here's the thing: when someone else is spraying it while they're saying it, the onus shouldn't even be on *you* to be the polite one. You just got spit on! But you know what? That's just the way the world operates—at some point in history, it was decided that it hurts a spitter's feelings if you wipe his or her saliva off your face. It's as though being spit on makes you the chosen one and it gives you the burden of transcending the situation. Maybe this weird social more came about because it was thought that you'd be drawing attention to a shortcoming. And maybe that's exactly what you *should* do—draw attention to it.

Why should you stand with spittle on your face like you are some kind of drooling idiot, when in fact you are not, the spittle isn't yours, and none of it is your fault? It's not like you have to make a big show of wiping your face off. Just do it. Odds are, if someone is speaking to the point of salivation, they are so invested in what they are saying that they won't even notice. They're probably not even listening to your replies.

How to Be in Line

Waiting in line can be one of the most annoying parts of someone else's day. There's no reason for you to make it even more annoying by being inconsiderate. One of the most important tenets of being a good line-waiter is to prohibit cutting. This includes being vigilant about others who engage in this loathsome practice. But don't take it too far. Speak up if it's happening in front of you, but stay out of it if it's happening behind you. (Otherwise, you're just being dramatic.) And there's no need to get too aggressive. You don't want things to escalate to a physical level.

Another key to good line etiquette is keeping it down. There's no reason why everyone around you needs to hear about your period, the kind of sex you had last night, or the fight you had earlier with your mother. *You* might think the events of your day are fascinating, but nobody else does. So don't get loud. Use low tones, put a cork in it, or, if all else fails, save it for your blog and/or Twitter feed.

Let's face it, the worst part about waiting in line is the boredom. But in this technological day and age, there is no reason why anyone should ever be totally bored again. Get a smartphone or an iPad or an iPod or a Discman or *something*. Play games. Listen to music. Check your e-mail. Read a book. Send texts. Shop for new apps. Check Facebook. We live in a glorious time when we don't have to actually sit with our own thoughts. Take advantage of that. Don't think of lines as something keeping you from the outside world. Use them as an escape to the World Wide Web.

How to Be Online

Stop crying.

Stop hating everything.

Stop hating everything just because other people like it.

Stop liking everything just because other people hate it.

Stop whining.

Stop complaining.

Stop picking every fucking little thing apart and refusing to give people the benefit of the doubt.

Stop fawning.

Stop policing people's language. (Sometimes *retard* IS the right word to use, and by arguing with us about it, you're retarding by keeping us from more important things.)

Stop being stupid.

Stop typing like you never learned how to spell.

Stop with all the inside jokes with people you've never met before.

Stop copying.

Stop embarrassing yourself.

Stop thinking that you're so important.

Stop thinking that you don't matter.

Stop visiting Perez Hilton. Why do you go there anyway?

Stop saying, "Must have a lot of time on your hands." Because *you* have a lot of time on your hands. That's why you're on the Internet.

Stop with the suggestions. If you want something made, make it yourself.

Stop asking strangers how to do things. Google it yourself and figure it out.

Stop getting outraged.

Stop being homophobic on YouTube.

Stop acting like you know everything.

Stop acting like you know nothing.

Stop buying so much crap.

Stop harassing people.

Stop bothering people with your life.

Stop trying to win the Tragedy Olympics. The Special Olympics are much cooler.

How to Be in a Car

Everyone, not just the driver, is responsible for safety in the car. Just because you aren't holding the wheel doesn't mean that you aren't carrying the burden of proper vehicular conduct. To paraphrase Judge Judy, cars are dangerous weapons. Sitting inside them is like sitting inside the barrel of a gun. Don't be a bullet or an idiot.

Don't cause unneeded distractions. By "unneeded," we mean any distractions, unless you're distracting the driver from plunging off a cliff or hitting something that they can't see because they're hitting the bong that you're holding in the backseat.

Look, anything we would have to say about this has already been handled more hilariously by the Crash Test Dummies (the actual dummies, not the band). Or in driver's ed. If you really have questions about this, go back to high school or the '80s.

 Aside: How to Pee in a Car

If you're a guy, this is simple enough: get a bottle and go. The bigger the mouth, the better—it's nicer if you can put your entire penis inside and unleash, as opposed to merely pointing the head over the mouth and hoping that you don't slip. Resign yourself to the fact that people in SUVs and trucks may see your wiener. Maybe you like that. In that case, make sure you go on every road trip with a full tank of gas and a full bladder.

If you don't have a penis, you cannot pee while in motion unless you are a passenger. If you are the driver, pull over. Now. Pee-filled passengers, you'll want to still have a bottle with you, but it will need a larger mouth. Gatorade or Snapple will do. Aquafina also made bottles that were even bigger than these. We're not sure if they still do, because honestly, who still drinks Aquafina?

The next step is to rip the cover off of something from the glove

---

compartment, like the car manual or an atlas—something a little sturdier and broader than your typical piece of paper. Fold it in half and make a crease. Take your seat belt off and scoot your butt up onto the back of your seat. Remove your pants and underwear and hold the paper you've just folded in a V-shape under your V. Put the bottle on the other side of the V/pee paper. Now pee, but be careful. Don't go full stream. (If you do, you'll just end up peeing all over the place, which you might do anyway, frankly.) Let things come out at a trickle so you can control the amount of fluid flowing down your makeshift funnel into your bottle. It's probably a good idea to have some kind of towel or T-shirt or backup underwear to sop things up before you put your butt back down onto the seat.

It should be noted that these bottles shouldn't be from lemon-flavored drinks because it may cause confusion and/or pee-drinking later. Apple juice is also a no-go, especially if you're dehydrated.

How to Be Good at Texting

W@ever u do, f u WAN2TLK, Nsure wen ur doiN it, u Rnt :*). dats d most literal wrd spew n XistenC—:*) txtN wl 1ly cre8 a mess dat Ull hav2 clean ^ 1s ur sober. LOL

jst sA w@ feels naked n d briefest wa posbL. *w* Treat yr ph lk a C=: n WIU. Feel fre 2 gt 6Y and/or 7K. It's deffo EZer W a QWERTY keybord, so f ur on a flip ph, or somit dat doesn't av a key per letta, YRYOCC. gt W d tyms!

Misunderstandings r comN n text-based Coms, so dnt gt so p*d dat u incriminate yrslf. hrs a gud rwl of thum: dnt txt NEfin u wudnt wnt read on jdge Judy.

dnt wori bout gramR (not dat ud f ur norml nor a ritR) or sp—jst gt yr point ax n B done.

Translation:

Whatever you do, if you want to talk, make sure that when you're doing it, you aren't drunk. That is the most literal word vomit in existence—drunk texting will only create a mess that you'll have to clean up once you're sober. Laughing out loud!

Just say what feels natural in the briefest way possible. (Wink.) Treat your phone like a penis and wrap it up. Feel free to get sexy and/or sick. It's definitely easier with a QWERTY keyboard, so if you are on a flip phone, or something that doesn't have a key for each letter, you're running your own cuckoo clock. Get with the times!

Misunderstandings are common in text-based communication, so don't get so pissed that you incriminate yourself. Here's a good rule of thumb: don't text anything you wouldn't want read on *Judge Judy*.

Don't worry about grammar (not that you would if you're normal and not a writer) or spelling—just get your point across and be done.

Translation No. 2:

Don't use text slang.

How to Be a Host

The cornerstone of being a good host is to make people feel welcome, no matter why they are in your home. This could mean providing entertainment, which includes but is not limited to food, drink, and ambiance. Frankly, there is nothing more entertaining than getting drunk. But if you're going to do this, match the value of the liquor you purchase with the value of the friendships that will be present. Go ahead and buy that gross Georgi vodka for the strangers who are going to blow through your house (hopefully before they blow chunks), but go whole hog and buy Grey Goose if you're liquoring up people you value.

By ambiance, we're referring to a situation in which people feel like they can be themselves. This means music or lighting or filling your place with guests that complement each other in some way. There's no science to this—it just requires a little bit of consideration. Don't slam a bunch of Type A's or a-holes into one room and expect it to go well. That's all we're saying.

If you're going to serve Jell-O shots and you don't want guaranteed vomit in your house, you should also serve some kind of bread-based food. Just a tip!

Don't take any shit from anyone. Never feel pressured into doing anything in your own house that you don't want to. Also, don't feel pressured into allowing anyone to do anything in your own house that you wouldn't do.

Also, don't take a shit. You'll set the tone, opening everyone else and their assholes up for similar bowel voiding.

Make sure you pay attention in the days leading up to your event for any vermin that may be in the house. Nothing will sideline a party faster than six-legged crashers. Or four-legged crashers. Or, if you live in Australia, two-legged-and-pouched crashers. Do any necessary spraying/trapping/taming well in advance of your guests' arrival.

And speaking of taming, make sure the animals that you want to live among (i.e., your pets) do not attack. Lock them up if needed, but use muzzles sparingly.

Mostly, just have fun, but—in the words that Cousin Shelly relayed to Anna Nicole from her adoptive mother—not too much fun.

How to Be Comfortable in a Club

Why on earth do sober people bother with clubs, unless they're on their way to getting drunk? Why would *any* clear-minded person want to be subjected to the sensory void of a noisy, dark, and packed atmosphere? You can have cheaper drinks, more in-depth conversations (and by that we mean conversations in which a person can make out the words another person is saying), and enjoy *better* music in far more comfortable environments. Like, say, your living room. Or whatever, a bar. A street corner. A bodega. Chili's. A bus stop. A desert. Literally anywhere.

So we advise you to get liquored up pregame and to bring a flask full of liquor to keep you from wanting to stab out your own ears and eyes and crawl out of your skin. We urge you to BYO because at clubs it seriously costs $20 for drinks that have a lower concentration of alcohol than your saliva after one homemade cocktail. Club drugs are dicier, and not that we're trying to help you into a K-hole or anything, but be aware that if you do decide to buy drugs at the club, you'll be paying an arm and a heart (attack), so that's best left to pregame activity as well.

Regardless of where your mind is, your ass and feet will understand that sitting down is the key to comfort. This will require either time or money. You'll either have to get there early and mark your territory, preferably by peeing on the upholstery, or hang around one area of the club long enough for a seat to open up. That's a lot of work just to sit down, but you could also secure yourself a seat by purchasing bottle service, at an average markup rate of 2,000 percent. We find this a ridiculous way to waste money and we wouldn't respect you any more as a result of it, no matter how rich you (or your parents) are.

In terms of female attire, we suggest wearing panties if you're wearing a short skirt. This is mostly so that you don't have to be worried about your vagina popping out the whole time—unless you get so wasted that you are no longer worried about anything. Or if you're the type of girl who would even consider going pantyless when wearing a short skirt, you might actually be pretty comfortable already. And please come over and hang out with us, because you're probably a good time, and if nothing else, we'll have someone to talk about in the taxi home from the club.

For ultimate club comfort, you may be surprised to learn how much marijuana can enhance the experience (for good, bad, and weird). But then again, you're reading this book, so you probably wouldn't be surprised about that at all. In fact, you may be reading this in a club right now. Tell the DJ we said hi and ask if he or she will play "Groove Is in the Heart." DJs love it when you make requests. If you take nothing else from this book, take that.

How to Be in the Face of a Backhanded Compliment

The hardest thing about handling backhanded compliments is identifying them in the moment. If they're good, they include some ambiguity that takes a minute to unpack. The best kind of backhanded compliment is like a delayed-action bomb that is designed to explode some time after impact, perhaps when the bomber has already walked away, presumably to spread his or her poison elsewhere. You may find yourself saying, "Hey!" to no one but yourself. If the delayed-action insulter had implied that you're pathetic, it turns out that he or she was kind of right.

The problem of responding to insults directly is that you don't want to seem petty. If the insult did take a while to reach you, then responding to it makes you seem not only petty, but petty and slow.

So if you don't catch onto the insult hurled at you right away, the best thing you can do is convey a vague sense of bitchiness toward the insulter for the rest of the evening/your life. If you do catch it in time, grow a pair and call that person out with a direct question: "What the hell is that supposed to mean?" People usually retreat when they have to explain themselves, unless they're on a reality show with cameras in front of them. Your confrontation will subvert their passive-aggression, and while they could pull off more malevolence with their slick tongue, they probably won't because they will be caught off guard. They were probably banking on a nuanced conversation layered with bogus niceties and barbed nastiness. So now you have the upper hand, which you can use to slap the shit out of them.

How to Be Quick with Comebacks

The problem with comebacks is timing—they usually come to you later, well after you've left the situation. If we had a dime for every time one of us has said, "I should have said...," we would have a pile of dimes at least as high as a pot-smoking gnome (isn't that cute imagery to think about?). Unfortunately, being quick requires time and patience. Unless you are a gifted genius like Judge Judy, we recommend you memorize this all-purpose list and never be shamed again:

Your mom. **Yeah, well, you smell.** Eat a dick. **Your breath suggests that you're talking shit.** Talk is cheap, but not as cheap as a hooker like you. **When God was handing out butts, he put one on your head.** If opinions are like assholes, yours has hemorrhoids. Didn't I see you on *Rock of Love*? **You're just jealous.** Stupid is as stupid stupids. **I'm not here to make friends.** You'd be more articulate if you were grunting. **You look like Meatloaf with a capital M, and you smell like meatloaf with a lowercase m.** You couldn't get laid if you were a paraplegic. **That's retorted.** You smell like a monkey and your butt is inside out like one, too. **Your idea of refinement is wine and smegma.** If hatin's your occupation, you should apply for unemployment. **I can see through your pants that your genitalia looks like a sandwich.** You think you're so smart, but that's only because you're not so good at thinking. **I've taken shits smarter than you.** My mom just died. **How old were you when you first ate lead paint?** I think you're mixing up being challenging with being challenged. **Talk to the hand puppet.** When's your *MAD* magazine cover coming out? **I'd tell you to call someone who cares, but pushing buttons seems like too much to ask.** I wonder what you look like naked—I'm very interested in medical mysteries. **Give it a rest—your brain needs it.** I don't shut up, I grow up, and when I look at you, I throw up. **You smell like Ke$ha looks.** Like sands through the hourglass, shut the fuck up. **Whatever's eating you must have**

low standards. Don't get your dog neutered—it might be the last time you ever see a pair of balls. **I know you are but what am I?** Tell your mom I hate her. **Do you have change for a dollar? I want to stick something in your panties.** When did you get removed from your host body? **Aw, you think you're people.**

How to Be at Work When You Want to Murder Your Boss

You're either going to have to suck this up or quit. *Sucking it up* does not mean "sucking up to your boss," it means "coping," and the best, most satisfying way of achieving this is by talking heaping amounts of shit about your employer. If your boss is terrible enough to inspire thoughts of homicide, chances are your coworkers have also noticed and will have plenty to say on the subject. It's a great bonding opportunity and a great way to meet new friends. There have been actual studies illustrating the way that shit-talking and mutual dislike brings people together. Look them up, but when you do, you'll probably have to Google a more benign phrase than "shit-talking."

All of this assumes that you can control your murderous impulses, no matter how strong they are. If you can't control yourself, you probably shouldn't be around anyone, ever. Quit your job and society now.

How to Be Able to Talk Again After Sticking Your Foot in Your Mouth

It's really appropriate to address this problem since it's happened so many times to each of us. Here we are again, talking again. The answer is: just keep going. Write a book if you need to. Just know that the more you keep talking, the less people will remember. Throw as much shit at the wall as possible with your mouth and see what sticks. It could be that your gaffe is what people take away from the conversation, or you could annoy them so much with your babbling that they just give up making heads or tails of you entirely and write you off as someone who talks too much. Talking too much is better than talking too stupid.

The worst thing you can do is to stop talking after you put your foot in your mouth, because you don't want your offending remark to be the last thing you say. It will echo in people's ears and reverberate through their souls. Depending on how egregious your slip was, you may want to apologize on sight—this is especially important if you just hurt someone's feelings and you know it. Because, no matter what you said, it's better to be stupid than mean. (To recap, our hierarchy here is: talking too much > talking too stupid > talking too mean.)

The thing is that everyone's been there and it sucks to be on the receiving end, but if someone isn't going to forgive your verbal mistake, he or she is a bigger asshole than you are and deserved whatever you said. In fact, he or she just did you a favor by making what you said not only okay but necessary.

How to Be When Someone Compares You to Someone You Think Is Unattractive

Angela Catsbury

If Rich were to write a memoir, it would be called *Not Being John Malkovich*, because he's been compared to John Malkovich on a frustrating number of occasions, by people who didn't know each other, and even lived on different coasts. That's the worst thing about it: there's clearly something to it if strangers agree. Regardless, they have no right to tell you that you look like someone who is cross-eyed and at no point was named one of *People* magazine's Most Beautiful People. He wasn't even named one of *People* magazine's Most Meh People. When people say this to you, you get the feeling that you're supposed to be flattered that they're comparing you to a celebrity. And while that says more about them than it does about you, it still hurts. No one wants to be compared to Ruth Gordon (you probably don't recognize her name because she isn't more attractive). Real talk.

And so, when someone does something so rude as to compare you to someone who isn't attractive by any standard, it's more than okay to call them on it. Rich has said, multiple times on multiple coasts, "That's offensive." He's explained to the person that he or she isn't the first to say this, so as to make them feel less alone. But they need to know that just because someone looks like a less-than-sexy celebrity doesn't mean that he should be treated like a less-than-sexy celebrity.

Besides, what on earth do people think they're accomplishing when they say things like that? The only good reason to tell someone he or she looks like a celebrity is to pay him or her a compliment and then sleep with him or her. When you tell someone he looks like John Malkovich, you're probably looking for him to not get inside your pants but rather your brain, and Rich can't do that because he isn't famous or a fictional character, nor does he have the requisite small door in his office, duh.

← *get it?*

How to Be Late All the Time Without People Hating You

The thing about being late is that when you finally do arrive, you have to acknowledge your lateness, apologize, and generally be nice. You don't have to be a publicist about things, but ingratiate yourself enough to make up for your negligence.

Ultimately, the way to get people to not hate you for being late is to not do it very often. Unless, of course, it's your thing. But in that case, you should really look into getting a new thing.

One good thing about being consistently late and the resentment that it may or may not provoke is that people's expectations of you are lowered. When that's the case, showing up someplace only five minutes late may impress people and you'll probably end up having a particularly nice time. This is true for many things, and sometimes it's hard not to make the argument that aiming low is the way to go. We won't even try now. Just be late until you aren't and everyone will love you even more.

How to Be a Good Liar

As Judge Judy says, if you're going to lie you have to have a good memory. You can't be a good liar if you're stupid. In fact, you can't be a good anything if you're stupid, except maybe a good lover and definitely a good stupid person. We do love a good stupid person as long as he or she is honest about it.

The thing about lying that's tricky is that you don't want to get caught and betray yourself with your own words. For that reason, you have to have a really good story worked out in advance and you have to commit to it. In fact, the more you can convince yourself of your own lie, the better off you are. Basically, this requires self-delusion bordering on mental illness. In order to truly deceive others, you must deceive yourself. Good luck with that.

While we believe that if honesty is the best policy then lying is the second-best policy, we really do not advocate going out of your way to be dishonest. Really, the phrase "good liar" is an oxymoron. We believe that the truth is good, period. What Judge Judy actually says is, "If you tell the truth, you don't have to have a good memory," and who really wants to be bogged down remembering tales? We have a hard enough time with facts like people's names and state capitals.

How to Be Around
Other People's Kids

Basically, you just have to feel your way through this one. However, don't feel the children, not even in a way that you think is "innocent." (The however to the however is if what you're feeling is teeth in your leg, get a tetanus shot.) Consider discontinuing your friendship with these children's creators (not God), assuming that you're even friends with them to begin with, or whatever. You're probably way too young to even have to really worry about this, and if you're not, you're probably friends with a teen mom, in which case: cool. Definitely be on your best behavior around other people's children if it means you will get to appear on reality TV. TV trumps friendship in most cases, you'll find.

The best way to be around other people's kids is to just avoid them. Use whatever you need to accomplish this: drugs and alcohol, for example, are not just poor man's vacations, they are vacations from children. If you can manage to pretend that all children are just very dimwitted little people (like, *Little People, Big World* little people), they will become infinitely more interesting to you, if not flat-out endearing.

Your level of tolerance for other people's children should match your tolerance for said other people. If you like the havers of these children, you must put up with their children. Silently. Do not say a word of negative observation or admonishment. However, if you are okay with burning bridges, feel free to say whatever you damn well please. A lot of people forget that children are children and have absolutely no say in the lives of adults. This is stupid. Children are the future, not the present or even necessarily a gift to anyone.

How to Be in a Public Bathroom

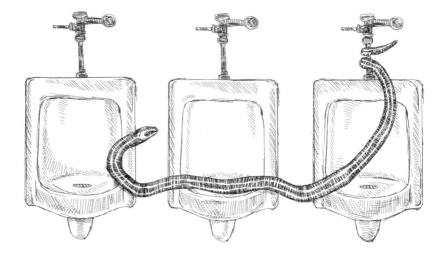

This question is different for boys and girls.

Boys don't tend to talk to each other in the bathroom unless they are trying to have sex with each other. But even then, no words speak louder than an erect penis. Rich has encountered multiple ones in his travels. Typically, the erect male will stand at a urinal and lean back so that he can display his erection decidedly but discreetly. It often takes a while for an onlooker to realize exactly what he's up to, but once it sinks in, there is no denying that his penis is ready to do work. As exciting as this may seem, don't fall for the bait of his masturbation.* We all know what happened to George Michael, and unfortunately, most of us don't have a record deal that would allow us to then get a song out of the situation. Plus, you're potentially exposing yourself to kids and that's truly fucked up, not to mention illegal. How to be in a public bathroom is not having sex.

Also, try to keep things as quiet as possible. See our section on "How to Be Gassy in Public" (page 223). Spreading your cheeks for the least amount of noise possible is easier if you're in your own stall. One time, Rich was at a urinal at work and a guy next to him farted and apologized. And then, to continue the conversation, the stranger asked, "Do you have to apologize if you fart at a urinal?" Funny that it was *after* he farted that he became concerned with etiquette.

Sometimes you might not want to wash your hands no matter what just went down. This is your prerogative; however, keep in mind that people will judge you based on your bathroom habits and talk about you behind your back. If you want to be known among your colleagues as the guy who doesn't wash his hands after he shits, that is your choice, but understand that this label will stay with you for life.

Also, keep in mind that you don't really have to be all that proper with your shit or general ass or even general genitalia, because you're in the dude's room and anything goes. Literally *goes*. It's kind of like a mini trip to jail, possible ass rape and all.

If you're a girl, it's understandable if you don't want to sit on a public restroom toilet seat. It's okay to squat and hover, but wipe up your mess when you're done because it's disgusting to leave a soaking wet seat behind. You are part of the problem that you are attempting to avoid. However, if you go into a stall and it is already covered in urine, you are not required to clean up someone else's mess.

If you're one of those hippie feminist types and you have a Diva Cup, try not to empty it out in one of the public restrooms that has a row of sinks. You're going to have to walk out in front of everyone and show them what your uterus just made. No one wants to see that. Your body, your choice, your uterus, your problem. Find a different bathroom and dump your waste.

Understand that if you are sharing space with women, they like to talk. They won't be afraid to ask for toilet paper from your stall if they don't have any in theirs or simply want to sample the variety that the bathroom offers. Be gracious about this. You never know when you will be without toilet paper yourself.

Take advantage of the anonymity of the public bathroom and let your ass exhale as it sees fit. No one's going to call you on your shit, because everyone is there to handle theirs. Literally. (Unless they just have to pee, of course.)

* And when a young, cute Latino guy in a Queens movie theater does it, it is indeed exciting, albeit distracting, because that is not the kind of show that Rich was there to see!

How to Be Honest Without Insulting Someone

Here's how *not* to do it: don't preface a disappointing truth with, "No offense, but…," or, "You know I love you, but…," or, "You're going to kill me for this, but…" That is stupid and does nothing to soften the blow.

The truth is that people don't like the truth. You can't control what other people will infer from what you're saying or what their reaction will be when confronted with something that seems obvious to you. It's really impossible not to insult people sometimes when *you're* just being honest, so really the best thing to do if you're so worried about hurting people's feelings is just not talk. Or just tell them what they want to hear and talk about the truth behind their backs. This isn't nice, but it will make them feel great. Even if they ask for an honest opinion, they probably don't want it. Do what's best for you and make your life as uncomplicated as possible. Besides, another name for "little white lies" is "manners."

If you find yourself in a situation where you must both be honest and refrain from insulting someone, like say you're forced at gunpoint to comment on the size of your clearly amateur assailant's gun, prepare to die.

How to Be Communicative with Your Parents When You're High

The thing about being stoned in front of your parents as opposed to being stoned in public is that so much more is at stake. Free food, Christmas presents, college tuition, in some cases shelter, in most cases respect. But we understand that there are times that you just have to be high to be around them. Other times, you'll have to be around them to be high. It's just what life throws at you.

The best way to communicate with your parents while you are stoned is to limit the communication as much as possible while not letting on that anything is up with you (i.e., highness). Say you're sick or need to use the bathroom a lot. Nothing gets a mom's compassion flowing like a child with diarrhea. Preface the conversation with how exhausted you are, regardless of the time of day. That's a great excuse for why your eyes are red and droopy and why you're a little loopy and possibly why you're rhyming so much. Extreme exhaustion is like being high, anyway, so if you seem a little punch-drunk, fatigue is a good explanation.

However, don't cheat yourself out of free entertainment. A lot of the goofy things that parents say will only seem more hilarious on weed. Lectures about your car insurance or direction in life or gossip about your aunts or entirely-too-long rundowns of what they just watched on TV that you already saw three years ago will all of a sudden be more tolerable, if not captivating. And, in the event that it is boring, weed will let you tune them out. This may not be the best strategy if they're expecting you to respond, but at least you'll be pain free in the moment. Let's live for today, people.

How to Be Wealthy and
Not Feel Guilty About It

While we don't really know what it's like to be "wealthy," there is certainly a point in your late twenties/early thirties where a divide forms between friends who start making more cash and friends who are still "starving artists." This makes for some awkward outings where you have to really compromise on cuisine or entertainment. Do you get nosebleeds or orchestra? First-run or dollar-theater? A champagne-room lap dance or a peep show? Compromise is an important part of friendship, but you don't have to go overboard and compromise your life.

You shouldn't feel guilty about doing things you can afford. You just might have to do them with other people who can afford them as well. Don't flash your good fortune in the faces of the have-nots. If you are feeling generous and want to invite someone who can't afford something and pay for them, knock yourself out...but be warned that you'll soon be beating yourself up over this. Paying other people's way gets really old really quickly, and so will the people benefitting from it—enough freeloading will suck the charm right out of someone. That is, unless they are giving you tremendous head, in which case they're probably sucking something else out of you.

Sex and Love
Non-Problems

How to Be Prepared
for Anal Sex

BÜTT SECTTS

1.

2.

3.

4.

How to Be Honest About the Penis Your Boyfriend Doesn't Know You Have

In the interest of full disclosure,* we will tell you that we're just as inexperienced regarding secret genitalia as the next guy or girl (but not as the next guy-girl). But, from what we understand, this is a problem facing at least one person on earth today, as we received in our inbox (literally, not vaginally) the following letter seeking our advice:

> I'm interested in your advice for a girl with a penis, in two scenarios.
> 1: Making out with a stranger at a party that could easily lead to hanky-panky.
> 2: Someone you've started dating, but before they get in your underpants.
> How would you handle the telling? Or would you not tell at all?
>
> Thanks!

We feel it is important to note that the first name of the person who wrote this is, ambiguously enough, Jean.

We love Jean, unique phrasing and all. We want nothing but the best for her, her penis, and her underpants. That is why, regardless of the hanky-panky potential, we recommend that Jean be up front about everything. A penis is a very difficult thing to hide, especially during hanky-panky. This is because blood fills the spongelike tissue in the girl penis, creating what is known as a stiffy. Stiffies know no gender identities. Protruding is protruding. And Protrudy is a wonderful name for a girl with a penis. Jean, we have someone we would like you to meet.

Honesty is the best policy when it comes to penises, which means lying is the second best policy. (See "How to Be a Good Liar," page 72.) Lying may be tempting, but it yields second-best results. Don't go for second-best, baby. Put your girl penis where your mouth is,[†] but don't bite off more than you can chew. And remember that this is a show-and-tell situation—don't bother telling if you don't plan on showing.

[*] Full disclosure is the answer for those asking, as well as those telling (i.e., us).
[†] If you're really that flexible, though, you don't need a boyfriend. Your life is full of options and you are busy enough before you even leave the house.

How to Be Aware Your Boyfriend Is Gay (If You Are Not)

What is gay? What is straight? What is bisexual? If these are questions you have, this is not the book for you. A dictionary is.

However, we don't begrudge you, your boyfriend, or anyone else out there who has questions about sexuality. Nowadays, people are wild and free with their lives and genitalia. People like to experiment by placing their genitals on things and in things. And also buttholes, which technically are not genitals but can be used as such. Anyway, the point is your boyfriend could easily be here today and gay tomorrow. And in the event that he is both here and queer, you don't have to get used to it.

You may have problems determining who's zoomin' who way before entering the bedroom. Whereas at one time signifiers a person chose like eyeliner, tight clothing, jewelry, piercings in the right ear, bags, tote bags, purses, clutches, chokers, skirts, high heels, hair products, leggings, pearls, fur, nail polish, waxed/plucked/threaded eyebrows, well-trimmed facial hair, big muscles, leather vests, sock-stuffed crotches, and flip-flops revealed everything you needed to know about sex with that person, metrosexuality and its dejected kid brother emo have been a scourge on gender normativity. That's fine. People can be however they want, except surprised when people don't get what the hell they're going for and they find themselves with some sexplaining to do.

Which is to say, the best way to be aware of your boyfriend's gayness is to say, "Are you gay?" (That also makes a great pick-up line for straight girls and gay guys. For the latter group, it cuts right to the chase. For the former, it weeds out the gay guys and it gives straight guys something to prove—and the best way to prove it is by having sex with a girl.) But maybe your boyfriend is not ready to give a definitive answer to that question. Or maybe the definitive answer is, "Depends on the day." Bisexuality is slippery, regardless of whether lube is involved. Sure, there are people who sleep with both genders throughout their lives, but for many, bisexuality is a transitional period. (Rich was once bisexual, except he wasn't.) But even if it's not transitional, it means that your boyfriend will want to fuck another guy at some point. And even if you don't think that's gay, you have to admit it's at least kind of queer.

Maybe your boyfriend isn't even ready to say the word *bisexual*. Does he request that you fuck him up the ass with a phallus? That would seem to be a gateway, particularly if the phallus has fake (or real) balls. Is he into veiny dildos? How lifelike is the penis head? These are minor points, but if he has a position on them, he's into dick, and eventually he could be into a person who has one. Is he sucking the phallus? Because that's not even about butt pleasure, and no, he does not have a prostate in the back of his throat. Is he one of those "straight" guys who likes masturbating to pictures of men? Or movies of men having sex? Some straight guys say that they just like to suck on penises. Real ones. (Have you ever heard of someone sucking on lollipops and saying they don't like candy?) How can you tell if a straight guy is lying about being gay? His speech is impeded by that dick in his mouth.

Girls, if you've experienced any of these situations, you're in a pickle (and no, that's not a euphemism for the penis your boyfriend wishes were in his mouth). Here's the thing: it's so hard. That's what she said, but also what he said, if he's gay.

How to Be Sexually Satisfied

Masturbate.

Masturbate always.

Masturbate on a train in the rain. Masturbate in a box with a fox.* Masturbate all over your green eggs and ham. Masturbate when you are having sex with another person, even if you are being penetrated by or penetrating that person. Touch yourself, touch your organs to their organs as though their organs are hands or inanimate.

If you're a girl, buy a Hitachi Magic Wand. The plug-in vibrators give you the most bang for your buck and fang for your fuck. (We're not being paid to say this, although we wouldn't turn down a check to elaborate. We're not above being whores, especially with sex toys.)

If you didn't get our point yet, we want you to play with yourself. Gals, don't think an orgasm you bring on yourself in the company of another is any less of an orgasm. That is hogwash and douchey. (By the way, don't douche; it's not good for you. But if you must, use hogwash.) An orgasm is an orgasm. (Orgasms, by the way, are chicken soup for the soul and word count.)

Guys, just fuck it like it's your hand. Whatever it is. If you are getting fucked, fuck your hand harder.

But maybe you are the type of fucker who gets off on giving pleasure. We've got news for you, sub-missy, you're still masturbating. You're manipulating the situation as if it's your genitalia. It's nice to be concerned about others, but when it comes to sex, the buck and fuck stops with you. Don't be a jerk-off; do jerk off.

---

*But don't touch the fox, because we don't advocate bestiality, especially with stranger animals, and let's face it, how many foxes do you know besides Michael J., Samantha, and the hotties in your circle?

How to Be a Virgin

The way to be a virgin is to have never had sex.

Failing that, if you want to *appear* to be a virgin, use Britney Spears's first years in the spotlight as your model. In other words, lie about it. In fact, make a point of lying about it even to people who don't ask you either way about your hymen. It's never too late to attempt to make chastity belts fashionable outerwear. And speaking of outerwear, dorkiness is the greatest cover of all. Rocking tinted red glasses will ensure that no one will mistake you for someone who is sexually active. Guffaw openly at nothing. Extol the virtues of e-mail. Make faces almost to the point of appearing to have a tic and refer to yourself as a "goob." Remember, when you brag about being a virgin, you're putting on a show of chastity. So jazz it up.

And another thing: exactly what constitutes virginity is mostly up to you. If you want to rationalize anal penetration as a virginity preserver, go right ahead. If you want to suck fifty dicks and consider yourself an untouched flower, hooray for you. Your body, your choice. If anyone wants to argue with you about it, make like the virgin you say you are, and refuse to fuck them. That'll show 'em.

How to Be a Slut

Use Britney Spears's Kevin Federline years in the spotlight as your model, and openly grab your partner's genitals through his or her pants and make out with him or her in public.

Make sure people see you doing it. This is crucial. The difference between sluts and other girls is openness—a slut will make sure you know how much she likes sex. Really, all it comes down to is a love of sex combined with a lack of politeness.

How to Be an Actual Human Around Your New Significant Other

This mostly has to do with farting and pooping and, if you're a gay male, other issues of the anus.

There will be a honeymoon period when love is in bloom and it smells like flowers are, too. You will also be in agony because you're holding in liters of gas you'd normally be emitting if you didn't have this fucking new and completely rewarding relationship. But the honeymoon must eventually end. And you can't keep leaving your newly loved one's apartment every time you have to poop. That's not practical or comfortable, and you're basically a ticking shit bomb. And also, maybe a ticking death bomb: among the complications that can arise from holding it in are constipation, IBS, and fecal compaction. Fecal compaction often leads to organ damage, loss of bladder control, death, and worst of all, having to dig up into your own ass to get yourself unclogged.

And by holding in your farts, you're basically making yourself a hot-air balloon, destined to start floating any minute. Try explaining *that*.

We understand that this is a delicate situation. Letting one go too early could be literally repellent. Despite what you may have learned in our entry titled, "How to Be Gassy in Public" (page 223), we urge you not to bend over and pull your cheeks apart during your first encounter with a stranger at a bar (also see: our "Hypocritical Oath"). Also, you must tread lightly at the beginning of your relationship when you're uncertain as to how comfortable your S.O.-to-be is with farting, lest you be defined by what comes out of your ass. The last thing you want someone saying about you is, "Oh, that girl I was dating? She farted. A lot. I hate her."

The best way to handle this is by crossing that bridge when you come to it. Gas will eventually slip out, and when it does, whether it's you or the person you're dating who does it first, you have to laugh. Even if you're crying at the time and purging your body of all that is inside. If a fart isn't a funny fart, it's just a fart, and that stinks.

To put it plainly: in order to break the ice, you must eventually cut the cheese.

Now, getting into poop:

Have you ever shit your pants? Try it, because it's so horrifying of a mess to clean up and smell that you will never want to even come close to doing it again and so you will defecate like a normal person: when you have to. You will start shitting at work whenever the mood strikes you. You will use the toilets of restaurants or clubs, if you must. Perhaps you will acquaint yourself with the great natural bathroom that is the ocean (beware, though: poop, like hope, floats). The primary goal of your life will become to never, ever, have feces in your pants again.

Pooping when you have to is an essential part of being a person. You cannot share yourself completely with another unless you are defecating regularly in his or her vicinity. Luckily, that person also has to shit, perhaps even right now, as you're reading this. If you're concerned with revealing your insides from an olfactory perspective, invest in air freshener or candles. Watch out for matches, though: while they almost magically eliminate the smell of shit with one strike, they smell so much like fire that they're bound to raise the question, "What's burning?" and then you'll still have to explain that you shit. Matches are a courtesy only for removing the smell, but they won't remove the impression that you pooped. Use sparingly.

Because *your* match is a person with a digestive system much like yours (unless it is an earthworm, but again, we don't advocate bestiality), perhaps he or she will be beyond understanding and want to turn normal bodily functions into a game of who can stink up the can worse. If that's the case, you deserve each other. Have fun with that.

How to Be Celebratory Yet Reserved on the Birthday of Someone You're Casually Dating

Rule of thumb/wallet: the amount of money you spend on someone matters, and nowadays they can look up pretty precisely what that amount is. If you don't want to seem overeager about the birthday of someone you started seeing or otherwise don't really care about, the best thing to do is buy him or her a present that says, "Hey. You're okay." Below is a list of suggestions for gifts that will make it seem like you're embracing the person while keeping him or her at arm's length.

- Pizza with birthday candles
- Picking up the check at a restaurant that has paper napkins
- A premium deck of cards
- Something monogrammed from the Lillian Vernon catalog
- Gourmet popcorn tin (the multiple flavor variety)
- Truffle oil
- A Yankee candle
- A stapler that looks like Pac-Man
- Temporary tattoos
- A book lamp
- A pair of shoe trees
- Fashion socks
- Hoop earrings
- Salt and pepper shakers in the shape of boobs
- A remaindered art book
- Condoms
- Spicy dice
- Flavored lube
- Edible panties
- Crotchless panties
- Furry love cuffs
- Anything from the sexy section of Spencer's Gifts
- A DVD that isn't from the Criterion Collection
- A disposable underwater camera

- A ride on a Ferris wheel or merry-go-round
- A small box of Godiva truffles
- A wooden bookmark
- A tie tack
- A tie rack
- Mittens
- A USB-powered character that has no purpose other than being cute
- A plant
- Shot glasses
- World's Greatest Something mug
- A flashlight
- Finger puppets
- A dime bag or two
- Fancy rolling papers
- Fancy ketchup
- Mascara
- Thank-you cards
- A snow globe
- A paperweight
- A funny apron
- A novelty nudie pen
- Anything that's novelty nudie
- A magazine subscription
- A clock
- A stopwatch
- Any time-taking or monitoring device
- A Fruit Bouquet
- A decorative pillow
- Concert tickets
- Movie tickets
- Fancy lip balm
- Coffee add-ins

- A remote control holder in the shape of a hand
- A giant remote control
- A Sing-a-ma-jig
- Ice cube trays that make ice cubes in fun and/or naughty shapes
- A lace-front wig
- Water wings
- A Swiss Army knife knockoff
- Fingerless gloves
- A lipstick holder with a mirror
- A Beanie Baby
- A decorative coffee cozy
- A sleeve for a pint of ice cream that prevents one's fingers from getting cold
- Personalized shoelaces
- A homemade coupon book with coupons such as "This coupon entitles you to a hug/blow job" (Note that the policy on doubling coupons is entirely up to you.)
- A mug with a mustache
- Gourmet jelly beans
- Any kind of repurposed LP record (a record bowl, etc.)
- Funny slippers
- Bunny slippers
- A nice key chain
- A money clip
- A monkey nip
- A tambourine
- Style Snaps
- An assortment of teas
- A footstool
- Insoles
- This book

How to Be When the Check Arrives on the First Date

Think about what you want the end result to be when the bill comes. If you're a straight man, even one who is dating a feminist, you should realize that you should pay, no matter what. If you don't pay for dinner, you'll have the debt of blue balls later. That's just how modern feminism works.

If you're a straight girl, you should offer to split the bill, even though you have no intention of actually doing so. Of course you can take care of yourself, but why pull out your wallet when someone can pull out his? It's more feminist, when you think about it, because you'll have more money for lipstick, abortions, and Bikini Kill reunion tickets. If the guy takes you up on the offer to go dutch, you'll probably still have sex with him, but it'll probably just be that one time. So again, he will end up paying.

If you're a gay man, it's honestly going to depend on whether you're a top or a bottom. Despite this being a first date, you almost certainly know your partner's top/bottom preference because (a) you've already fucked him, or (b) he mentioned it in his Grindr profile. Tops are probably more egalitarian and open to whatever, ironically enough, whereas bottoms think they own the place and demand that you pay for them like their active assholes have bought them entitlement. Whatever. Just do it—because like a straight man, you'll pay either way. If you're both versatile, the concept of going dutch was practically invented for you.

If you're a lesbian, you're on your own. As a straight woman and gay man, we don't have experience with lesbians in this context. Although Rich dated a lesbian back in college, where first dates amounted to sitting together on a dorm couch. For Rich's birthday, she bought him a Jeanette Winterson book that he'd already read and that they'd already discussed.

How to Be a Sideline Ho

We don't advocate cheating, but we understand that it happens. In the words of the late, great Whitney Houston, it's not right, but it's okay. And that brings up a bigger point: the subject of cheating has been an essential part of soulful music. Everything you need to know on the subject can be found on the radio. Here are some essential tips on fooling around from the great thinkers who have reflected and shaped our lives:

- Fool around and you'll be doing it without receiving benefits, house keys, pillow talk, being held at night, or the supposed honor of making that person's breakfast (Monica, "Sideline Ho").
- Creep: keep it on the down-low (TLC, "Creep").
- You can forget about tomorrow or even the concept of foresight because you just have the night (Shirley Murdock, "As We Lay").
- You're on borrowed (or actually, stolen) time, so keep track of it, even when you're in the middle of makin' love (Atlantic Starr, "Secret Lovers").
- You're going to have to face that you're last on his or her list, because he or she has his or her family and they need him or her there (Whitney Houston, "Saving All My Love for You").
- You can never have it all, you'll have to hit a wall, inevitable is withdrawal (Amy Winehouse, "Tears Dry on Their Own").
- Speculation will bring you stares (Xscape, "My Little Secret").
- Be an improvement over every aspect of that person's significant other and have a chip on your shoulder about being considered second-best (Pleasure P, "Boyfriend #2").
- Be aware that you'll probably get pregnant or get someone pregnant because drama has a way of creating more drama/babies (Usher, "Confessions Pt. 2").
- You might as well embrace your shamelessness (Meshell Ndegeocello, "If That's Your Boyfriend [He Wasn't Last Night]").

- Take him/her, shake him/her, ring him/her all out, and show him/her what it's all about (MC Luscious, "Boom! I Got Your Boyfriend").
- You're never going to be able to dance again—guilty feet have got no rhythm (Wham! featuring George Michael, "Careless Whisper").
- You can't be seen with him, but you don't care, because in a room behind a door, no one but y'all are there (Naughty by Nature, "O.P.P.").
- Study popping and dropping to provide a superior alternative to his or her significant other in those areas (Jacki-O, "I Got Your Boyfriend").
- Brace yourself for the holidays—you gotta always be by yourself 'cause that's the time when the families get together, all the in-laws come to visit, so he has to stay home and play the part of the good, faithful husband (Millie Jackson, "[If Loving You Is Wrong] I Don't Want to Be Right").
- Call up, ring once, hang up to let your insignificant other know you've made it home (Stevie Wonder, "Part Time Lover").
- Meet every day at the same café with a good jukebox (Billy Paul, "Me and Mrs. Jones").
- You're going to have to buy tickets to D.C. if you want to hold hands publicly (John Legend, "She Don't Have to Know").
- You are a part-time love, but don't be a part-time fool (The Soul Children, "I'll Be the Other Woman").
- Always make sure there is a closet with enough room to fit you inside, so that you can watch a multipart soap opera play out as a result of the drama that comes from sneaking around (R. Kelly, "Trapped in the Closet").

How to Be a Power Bottom

We are of the philosophy that anal sex is such an intense activity that any bottom is a power bottom. But we understand every activity has a hierarchy. There are skydivers and there are naked skydivers. There are tightrope walkers and there's that French guy from that movie. There are moviegoers and there are theater jumpers. There are teen wolves and there are van surfers. There are hot dog eaters and there is Takeru Kobayashi. There are singers and there are yodelers. There are couponers and there are extreme couponers. There are dogs and there are rabid dogs.

That said, all social interactions involve give-and-take, but just because you're taking doesn't mean you don't have something to offer. In this case, you're offering a part of you that is delicately lined and prone to disagreement: your butthole. Wikipedia says that a power bottom is someone who aggressively enjoys receiving anal sex, but a dick in your ass is so consuming that there is no passive way to enjoy it. There's aggressive enjoyment and then there's anal rape. There's no gray area, and if there were, it would probably be brown anyway.

There are connoisseurs of anal sex to whom no amount of fucking is enough, and no penis is too big. If you aspire to be one of them or just are, perhaps fisting is for you. Or you can try using a series of increasingly large butt plugs that will stretch out your anus to the point where it can no longer stretch back and the butt plugs that were once elective are now a necessity.

How to Be with a Guy
Who Used to Be Gay

Everybody has a right to change something about themselves that they aren't happy with, but the thing about sexuality is that by definition it (almost) always involves someone else. Many young ladies have asked us about men that they're dating who used to be gay. But here's the thing: that implies that sexual orientation is a choice that someone makes, and we don't think that's true. We understand that there are people who consider themselves bisexual and spend extended periods of time with mostly people of one sex. But for someone to renounce their former homosexuality raises all kinds of red flags where rainbow ones used to fly.

Ultimately, what we're saying here is that you can be with a guy who says he used to be gay, but chances are he'll be gay again another day. And if he isn't, you'll spend your life waiting for him to be. And then he'll get to his Keyshia Cole point and say, "I might as well have been gay for all that you accused me of it." God, your relationship seems really hard (unlike his penis when it's around you) and sad (*like* his penis when it's around you). We don't envy you. Entering into this kind of relationship is like living at the foot of a volcano. No one knows when he'll blow . . . a dick.

At the very least, you'll probably spend hours and hours talking about his past and how it compares to his present and whether his past is an issue or will be one in the future or what his past could have been or how the future will change his past if at all. Your present will be wrapped up in tenses, and that will make for tension. Maybe you don't have much going on, or maybe you don't have much in common. At least, this will give you something to talk about and care about. But no matter what, this won't be an easy ride, and that goes beyond the questionable hardness of his dick. You're looking at an investment of time and drama. If that's what you want, marry an ex-gay today.

To paraphrase Bell Biv DeVoe, what we really mean to say is: never trust a fucked butt and a smile.

How to Be Safe but Not Sorry, Sexually

Welcome to the '90s.

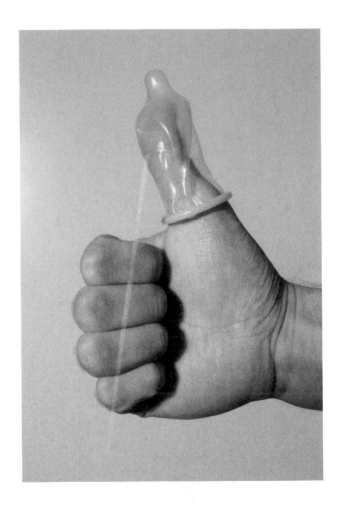

How to Be Sensitive While Acknowledging Your Partner's Recent Weight Gain

This is a very sensitive topic, because it's very difficult to discuss how someone's appearance deviates from what society considers beautiful or normal without offending that person. Of course, there's a larger issue here (pun intended, obviously, or we wouldn't have included it): health. But let's get real—you wouldn't notice someone's cancer unless a tumor distorted his or her appearance. So don't pat yourself on the back for your concern regarding your partner's internal well-being. The only reasons you know about his or her health being jeopardized in the first place are superficial reasons. You shallow asshole.

Just kidding. We all care about looks, especially those of someone we're supposed to be attracted to. Because duh—this is some by-definition shit. When his or her physique changes midrelationship, you feel like you bought a ticket to see Louis CK and when you showed up, you got Gallagher. There are few things more American than shaking your fist while screaming, "False advertising!" and we believe that politics should always be left out of the bedroom.

All of this is to say that this is a delicate situation, which you may have surmised when we described it as a "sensitive topic." When it comes down to it, in the long run, when all is said and done, all in all, bringing up the rear, bottom line, in conclusion, to sum it up, ultimately and at the end of the day, it's your sex life. You have to be proactive to get what you want, as Madonna has taught us. But you don't want to be so offensive that you're not going to get laid ever again.

As in all areas of life, the best way to approach this is to lead by example. Your significant other will smell hypocrisy if you're telling him or her to lose weight while you have Dorito breath. If you haven't already, put down the chips, get your ass in the gym, and lead a healthier lifestyle into which you can incorporate your partner. Studies that we read at some point suggested that weight loss really sticks when you do it as a couple. And once you've done that, you can open up a dialogue, but hopefully with more finesse than that which you used to open up that bag of Doritos.

When broaching the subject, do not come right out and say, "Hey, fatso." Don't even say, "Hey, heavier-so." Instead, discuss how you think it would be mutually beneficial to become healthier as a couple. If that doesn't work, you may have to be more blunt, depending on the severity of the weight gain and how much it's affecting you and your attraction. The real bottom line (and it's a big bottom...line) is that one person's unrequited attraction affects the whole.

There's no joke or pun to wrap this up with, that's just what it is. Have a miserable life.

How to Be Incestuous

Don't.

How to Be Married

Unfortunately, in order to be married in most states—the kind of marriage that is recognized by the U.S. government and gives you special privileges like health insurance or deciding whether or not to remove your spouse from life support—you'll have to be in a heterosexual relationship. We hope this changes in the near future. However, for the time being, we're going to talk about marriage in the legal sense because, as we see it, the legality of the institution is the only thing that separates it from a civil union or a life partnership.

Really, the only way that you can be married is if you don't get divorced. So, if you want to be married, do what you need to in order to avoid divorce at all costs. This could include measures as drastic as couples therapy or even tying your spouse to the bed and never letting him/her leave the home, or it could be as simple as conceding the remote control in a pop-cultural power struggle. Sometimes it just means giving more blow jobs. Other times it means having to confront—and ultimately be okay with—skid marks in underwear that do not belong to you. You'll always have to share everything. And you'll have to let go of the concept of "mind your own business." You'll have to be cool with only having sex with one person for the rest of your life, unless of course the two of you make some sort of "arrangement" (in which case, you seem to have this under control). You need to get used to the idea of forever, because even though "as long as you both shall live" doesn't necessarily mean "infinity," it's as close as you're going to get. And that's a mighty long time. (Hopefully!)

But the upside is that you won't die alone. Well, unless you're traveling separately and one of you goes down in some horrible plane crash. Hopefully it's your spouse and not you. And hopefully you're young enough to meet someone new and start over again. In which case, all of these rules about marriage will still apply. Good luck in your endeavors.

How to Be When You Queef During Sex

Be like this:

Of all the embarrassing stuff that can happen during sex—urine leaks, unwelcome fingers in intimate places, saying the wrong person's name—queefing is right up there at the top of the list. It may be even more taboo than farting. But you know what? That's only because it's something that guys can't do, so they're freaked out by it, which in turn makes women feel weirder about it. But really, aside from it sounding funny, there's nothing gross about a queef. It's just an emission of air from the vadge that "does not involve waste gases and thus often has no specific odor associated," according to the Wikipedia page about "vaginal flatulence."

Women are most susceptible to queefing when switching up positions during sex, especially when going from an extended period of doggy to missionary. If you have enough experience to be able to feel a queef coming on, one method for avoiding it is to do a sort of scoot/twitch/hip-switch thing to try and get the air out of there relatively inaudibly before the penis is reinserted.

But sometimes there's nothing that can be done about it; you can't get control of it, and it's unstoppable and seemingly goes on forever. And then when you think it's stopped, some more squeaks out. It's stupid to be embarrassed about it, but when you're fucking someone for the first time, and your vagina is performing a symphony, it's kind of hard to not cringe with your whole being.

The best way to deal with queefing is to simply laugh. Because if you try to ignore it, it just gets *weird*. And then you might lose your concentration and be unable to come. And you never want to let manners get in the way of your orgasm.

How to Be About STDs

This isn't a question of how to be, it's one of where to be, and the answer is in the doctor's office. And in most cases, once you're out of there, how to be is to be taking penicillin. (Or whatever your doctor prescribes.)

But what about certain incurable STDs? Well, it's not just about your attitude, but society's in general. In a 2007 WebMD poll about relationships, genital herpes was ranked the second-highest social stigma—HIV came in first—ahead of gonorrhea, mental illness, obesity, substance abuse, and cancer. According to the Centers for Disease Control, one in five adults have had a genital herpes outbreak. And the stats are even higher for women (approximately one in four). In fact, one of the two authors of the book you have in your hands has genital herpes. So why all the shame? Given that herpes is so common, that it can be contracted while wearing a condom, and that outbreaks are for the most part few and far between (and for some of us, never recur), we're offended that people are, well, offended by our infection that is comparatively so benign.

Here's the thing: herpes is actually in the same virus family as chicken pox, which is an illness no one is embarrassed about. When you're in a room of forty people, statistics show that eight to ten of them will probably have some form of herpes, so you shouldn't feel shame, you should feel on trend. Sure, your Valtrex prescription isn't something you'd hang up on the fridge with pride, but you don't have to feel bad about it, either.

How to Be into Period Sex

If you are a woman:

Tracie ran into the infamous sexpert Dr. Ruth, at a Cosi in Manhattan. She is someone infinitely more qualified than we are to answer this problem. This is Tracie's story:

> I don't really remember how I exactly put it, but I mumbled (so as not to alert the other diners what a sicko I am) something about the pros and cons of period sex. 'Cause I don't know about anyone else, but I get crazy horny on my period. Not like the first two days when I'm like all diarrhea and cramping and it's superheavy, but like around day three or four. It can be difficult to talk guys into fucking you then, especially if you don't know them that well. Some dudes just get freaked out by it, and don't recognize it for what it is— extra lube.
>
> Anyway, whatever I said didn't faze Dr. Ruth at all. Without missing a beat, she said, "Just use a diaphragm to make it less messy." She cupped her hands up to illustrate, "It will catch it and keep it up there." Then she smiled, looked back down at her book and literally shooed me away with her hands. Best. Dismissal. Ever.

And here's an added bonus: the concentration of blood down there can trigger extra-intense orgasms for women, and climaxing during menstruation can relieve cramps. That's quite the beneficial circle for your cycle.

If you aren't into period sex out of courtesy for your partner, don't even give him the chance to rag on your rag. Get him excited without revealing your uterine situation. Save your reveal for when his boner is at the point where it has to fuck, and then, once he discovers that you, in fact, have your period, tell him, "I don't mind if you don't mind." If he does mind, he's a bigger vagina than you'll ever have.

If you are a man:

Just do what the woman wants and you will get laid. Plus, aren't you supposed to like sticking your dick into warm and gooey things?

How to Be in an Office Romance

In a word, don't.

Work is the one environment that you can't get away from without putting yourself at risk for poverty and/or starvation. You can turn your back on your family, you can leave your spouse (and live with family, provided that you haven't already turned your back on them), you can cut off friends, you can go to a different post office, but your job is your job. Of course, you can also leave your job, but ugh, what a nightmare that always is. Tying up loose ends and negotiating shit and e-mailing your new contact information to anyone who may be able to help you at your new position and rolling over your 401(k) and saving all of your important work information is such a hassle. Also, maybe you'll hate your new job and find yourself turning to a new coworker to use sex as a coping mechanism, and then you're the office bicycle. You're screwed in more ways than one, because when your romance (if that's what you want to call it) dries up, you still have to work there and then you're going to feel all weird because you just got that job and leaving so soon will be uncomfortable. And then you run the risk of using even more sex to cope. It's a circle more vicious than an irritated asshole.

So, yeah, don't.

But let's say there are actual feelings there and this isn't just the sexual equivalent of a coffee break. The danger in this is that given the circumstances, it's likely that only one of you will have taken on the emotional responsibility of this relationship. Hopefully, it's not you, although let's face it: if you're reading this entry and still paying attention this far down the page, it is and you are sad. For one of you, going from the boardroom to the bedroom is nothing but an extension of happy hour. In most cases, work is too full of stimuli to breed actual commitment. Or at least, that's what we think because that makes sense right now.

Miracles happen, and regardless of how distracting the environment, sometimes love finds you amid the QED reports, petty cash, and

135

giant jars of M&Ms on your boss's desk. This is the worst scenario for *everyone else* in the workplace. Contrary to what you may believe, no one else falls in love with you falling in love. Think back to Jim and Pam on *The Office* and how lame they became when they fell in love. They became drooling baby peddlers whose single function was to remind their coworkers how perfect and happy their lives became under those fluorescent lights. It's enough to drive everyone around them to drink or distract from the distractions with office romances of their own. We've already advised against that, so please keep that in mind when you want to infect everyone else with your happiness.

Also, let's keep it professional, and confine such dalliances to office holiday parties.

How to Be Practical About
Your Violent Fantasies

The most important thing in sex and life in general is not to kill anyone (including yourself), on purpose or otherwise. That being said, for some people (NOT US), it can be arousing to come very close. Choking, smacking, punching, making people vomit, making yourself vomit, cutting, inserting, fisting, twisting, turning, and burning are all activities people enjoy doing while naked and/or to their naked parts and the naked parts of others. We don't judge this (publicly), but we do advocate for safety and a safe word. In fact, sometimes by the time the safe word comes up, it is already too late (in theory), so maybe you should have a safe sign that would signal the imminent safe word. This is a lot to think about when your balls are in a vise or your vagina lips are being stretched like taffy by clothespins, but a thinking sadomasochist is a responsible sadomasochist.

Obviously, acting out your violent fantasies requires a consenting partner or partners. This throws the concept of rape fantasy out the window, as that would require someone who wasn't consenting, but whatever. How you negotiate your need to have forcible sex with someone who doesn't want to is your business (as long as you aren't actually doing that), and fantasies are all make-believe by definition anyway, so whatever squared.

And actually, whatever to this whole thing, because the safest way to realize your fantasies is to watch other people do it in porn and masturbate and then you won't even want to have sex for at least some period of time and you can fold your socks or read more entries in this book.

Safety first; *How to Be* second.

How to Be in an
Online Relationship

This entry is not about finding a mate online, because that's easy enough to do already. Go turn on your computer and a dating service will come to you. It's simple science. Instead, we present the top twenty ways to be when you've already entered into a relationship with a person you met online but with whom you have yet to socially consummate your relationship.

1. Don't give out your bank account information.
2. Don't give out your Social Security number.
3. Don't send money orders.
4. Cease all communication if the person is e-mailing about being a Nigerian prince.
5. Send flattering but real pictures of yourself.
6. Understand that pictures you receive might not really be of the person with whom you're in a relationship.
7. Don't send naked pictures of yourself (or at least not naked pictures with your head in them).
8. Don't reveal too many things about yourself that you might regret later.
9. Don't disclose your family members' names.
10. Don't feel required to even reveal your own last name.
11. Do Google-stalk them if you get the other person's last name.
12. Understand that the longer you carry on without meeting, the more this is becoming a virtual game. But that's okay if that's all you want. If that's *not* what you want, understand that you're essentially wasting your time.
13. If you're going to keep things in the virtual world, then do that: don't use the USPS for any mail or gifts. Send e-cards.
14. Never feel indebted to this person.
15. Remember that you can always turn off this relationship by turning off the computer.

16. Don't be afraid to ask questions. It's okay to be afraid of the answers.
17. Talk about your online relationship to your real-life friends as little as possible. You don't want the added hassle of people judging you, because they probably will.
18. It is okay to become emotionally invested as long as you remain aware that you will most likely look back on this and wince.
19. It is more than fair to date around and have more than one of these relationships if you need to. There are many fish in this virtual sea. Why not shove your pole at a few?
20. Don't let your weird sense of guilt about somebody who's a stranger you met on the Internet convince you not to follow our advice.

How to Be When You Run into Your Ex with His or Her New Partner

Provided that you are a generally well-adjusted individual, this will depend largely on how much time has passed since you were with your ex. If it's been five years and you fall to pieces on sight, you need therapy or more therapy. Still, any brush with the past can put even the emotionally stable in a situation that ranges from awkward to painful. There are certain things you can do to minimize any weird feelings of humiliation that may result from such encounters. Situations like these are the exact reason why you should look your best each and every time you leave the house. If you're a female, this means wearing makeup. If you're a guy, this means not wearing makeup unless you now want your ex to think you're "like that." It's your image, go crazy.

It is probably best not to dredge up the past too much, so if the situation can be handled with a distant smile and wave, go for that. This way, you don't seem rude but you also don't have to talk to your ex and that new hussy he or she has adopted. However, sometimes you may find yourself in an elevator or in line with your ex. You may be confronted with him or her or them face-to-face (-to-face) and *you'll* look like the weirdo if you retreat or attempt to ignore.

The most important thing to remember in this is that the onus is on your ex to introduce you to his or her current partner. Do not say, "Well, *whooooooo's* this?" That will make you look like you care and make you sound like an owl. Really, the key to this exchange will be coming off like you do not care about anything in it. Don't be a douche bag about it and don't represent yourself as completely apathetic or your ex will wonder if somehow the absence of his or her love has made your essence frigid. Be the impressive person you are, but don't look like you're trying to impress. It's a fine line. See below for some examples of how to walk it.

- Compliment something the ex's current flame is wearing, because that makes you look thoughtful and above it all.
- Talk about career developments in vague terms—just make sure it sounds like something they would want to be doing.

- Avoid looking self-absorbed by asking questions that seem considerate but are vague enough to avoid prying. Examples include, "How's your family?" (which has the added benefit of digging at the current flame a little because it shows you knew him or her like that) and, "Who are you wearing?"
- Bring up *your* current flame only as needed, with as few words as possible. Basically, any situation that would have you lie by *not* mentioning your new S.O. is best handled honestly, but you don't want to seem too eager to show that you are just as capable of moving on as your ex is, because that eagerness will undermine your perceived capability.
- Don't get into pop culture or general interest because, seriously, how long are you going to be there? You can overlook this rule if you are stuck in a nonmoving elevator and literally have nothing else to talk about.
- If the subject turns to the weather, you will know that the conversation is over. Leave.

How to Be When Warding Off Unwanted Advances

Make like Webster in the antimolestation PSAs of the '80s and:
SAY NO.
AND GO.
AND TELL...all of your friends about the douche bag that just tried to sleaze up on you. He or she gave you the gift of a story, which is a nice present.

How to Be Fuck Buddies

We do not endorse friends-with-benefits relationships. They are unsustainable and we'd hate to see you waste your time. As Ashton Kutcher, Natalie Portman, Justin Timberlake, and Mila Kunis taught us, one person always takes on the emotional responsibility, leaving things extremely awkward for the other person, who thought the deal was that there wasn't going to be any emotional responsibility. There's just something about the combination of genitals that makes some people feel close. Fair enough, we guess.

Basically, you have to choose between the fuck and the buddy. You can't be both. You're better off having repeated sex with someone you hate, because there at least will be no love lost when things go south, which they always do. And that is our point. It can only go downhill from going down on someone that you have a mutually beneficial relationship with.

If you're into having sex with someone repeatedly that much, you should be with them for real. And if there are reasons that you don't want to be with them for real, stop having sex and find someone else to have regular sex with. That's what everybody wants, anyway. At least that goes for most people who aren't poly or whatever. It's not that we're saying that you have to marry everyone you fuck or that you can't be promiscuous, but if you do it repeatedly with someone who you don't want to make it official at all with, get ready for a hassle, either from them or from your insides. Get ready for your tolerance to be as fucked as your genitals.

How to Be After a Threesome

The primary thing to remember is just to be as affable with every party as possible, so as not to let on that one person of the two that you were having sex with was favored, even if he or she was. You just shared something private and personal (fluids) and that leads to vulnerability all around. You don't want one member of your threeway to feel like he or she is somehow less than everyone. He or she could go crazy, and you know that he or she is already wild because he or she just took part in a threesome.

Unless you're into the polyamory thing, you don't really have to work at keeping a relationship going with these other two people. Use your sense and good manners and be polite without getting too close. Or, if you already are close to one of them (say, your boy- or girlfriend), reassure him or her that you enjoy having sex with him or her far more than with that other person that you probably just—for variation alone—had way more fun having sex with. This is your little secret that you can masturbate to.

And so the best way to be after a threesome is in a onesome.

This advice would also apply to a one-on-one one-night-stand situation, except for the fact that now two people know sexual things about you and one of those things is that you are at least amenable to the idea of having sex with more than one person at a time. Big whoop. Who isn't? Some people, but they're probably Republicans with kinkier things to worry about.

How to Be in Bed with Another Person

If you are looking for advice on getting another person into bed with you, this is not the chapter for you. Look elsewhere in this book, look inside your soul, but most importantly, look on Craigslist and order a hooker. This entry is all about what happens after you've made that hooker a housewife or househusband; we offer tips for sharing space in the nest inside your love nest. Unless you are an actual bird (in which case: congrats on your literacy), we are referring to your bed, of course.

Alarms: There's no worse way to spend a morning than in that twilight between sleep and consciousness inflicted by someone next to you pressing the "SNOOZE" button repeatedly. Think about that when you're pressing "SNOOZE" a million times while lying next to your significant other. Because it's hard to be perfect, though, one way to soften this terrible blow is by waking up to pop music, via CDs, MP3s, or the radio, or by making your own ringtone that you assign to an alarm on your iPhone like one of the anal-retentive authors of this book does. This, obviously, depends on your partner's taste, and regardless of that, he may not want to hear the first thirty seconds of Mariah Carey's "I'm That Chick" every day for about two years, just to use a random example. But hey, it's worth a try.

Blankets: We advise you to apply Barney's approach to blocks and dolls and toy fire engines and shit, and adopt the philosophy that sharing is caring. This includes, but is not limited to: proper blanket distribution, agreeing on the level of coverage (Are you using a top sheet? Quilt or comforter? Does your duvet have a cover?), and not cutting off access to any of those layers by lying on top of them. When you are in bed with someone, you forfeit your right to lie on top of the blanket if that person wants to be underneath it. However, you may find yourself sharing a bed with someone who is not as considerate as we are. Poor you. In that case, we recommend enforcing fairness by any means necessary, including force. Start with your elbows.

Breathing: Since you are an organism (but not an orgasm, because orgasms can't read and you're reading, which is how you can tell the difference between yourself and an orgasm), you must breathe. Everyone does; everyone has their own style, and everyone needs to deal with everyone else's method of oxygen intake and carbon dioxide output. However, they do not need to deal with it up close. Keep your breath out of other people's business and refrain from sleeping face-to-face.

Eating: Come on, it's so gross, and you know what's even grosser? When you are the person who didn't eat in bed but are confronted by remnants including, but not limited to: wrappers, crumbs, sprinkles, ice-cream cake crunchies, apple cores, apple seeds, apple chips, cheese rinds, pork rinds, melon rinds, fried chicken skin, and semen.

Farting: If you don't know your significant other well and are still attempting to keep up the illusion of a gas-free lifestyle (see How to Be an Actual Human Around Your New Significant Other, page 101), you'll want to empty your ass as completely as possible before getting into bed with him or her. However, since hopefully you're at that point in a relationship in which you are openly farting, don't let sleep knock you off course. Just make sure you don't back that thang up into your partner because it's fucking disgusting to be spooning someone and get a dollop of fart in return. There's also that weird as-seen-on-TV product called the Better Marriage Blanket, which is supposed to absorb the smell of gas before it can ever hit your partner's nose. However, this is primarily for straight people, since gay people can't have marriages in most states, let alone better ones.

Grooming: While personal hygiene can make one prettier, it's not necessarily a pretty business. And you know what? It's *your* business, so keep it out of confined, shared spaces. Because when it comes down to it, the crap that bursts out from between your teeth when flossing is nothing more than decayed food and rancid meat. So don't make other people sleep on that, unless you're medieval or something.

Lights (camera, action): In the event that the two of you disagree on the ideal lighting situation as you are going to sleep, the rule is that the person who wants the lights off wins because sleeping in the dark is what normal people do. Of course, this rule can be waived if the person who wants the lights on is considerably stronger or just more physically intimidating. However, if there's some bullshit reason that person wants the lights on, like a fear of the dark, the scaredy-cat should recognize the fact that he is at least on a team of two, and two heads are better than one unless what's coming out of the dark is a two-headed monster. In the event of complete stubbornness, sleeping masks can be employed, but it kind of sucks to fall asleep with something strapped to your face, so the light-loving scaredy-cat wins in multiple ways and that sucks even more. In other words: we don't know, figure it out yourself.

Nightmares: This stuff is in your head (literally) and you should do everything you can to keep it there until the morning when you can laugh about it with your partner instead of getting him or her scared, too. If you are both in a state of fear, it will make it much harder to be strategic and rational when that two-headed monster walks through your bedroom door.

Pets: We vote yes to pets on the bed, within reason. If your animal is particularly dirty, prone to standing on your genitals, or a lizard, you will probably want to keep them from walking on you/your bedding. Essentially, our belief is that only cute pets belong in bed, and pets are at their cutest when they are clean and not lizards.

Positions: Positions don't matter unto themselves, just as long as they coordinate with each other. It might be weird to sleep in a 69, but our philosophy condones it, so go crazy.

Snoring: We would never ask you to lose weight, but Rich will tell you that when *he* lost weight, he snored infinitely less. Take from that what you will. Quitting regular drinking, smoking, drugging, and other addictions can help with this problem, too. Basically, the healthier you are, the less rattle you give off. Surgery is a personal decision, but we believe it's a drastic measure and far more expensive than the pain delivered from your partner's occasional punch. If you find yourself having to deliver a punch or shove to get your partner to shut the fuck up while you're trying to sleep, just think of it as DIY surgery and laugh about how much money you saved by not going to med school.

Touching: This should be handled on a case-by-case basis, but when in doubt, keep your paws to yourself and your overgrown toe-nails from grazing the feet and back of your significant other.

TV: We both feel strongly about the healing powers of falling asleep with the TV on, but then again, we are both pop culture–addicted bloggers who don't have enough waking hours to take in all of the TV we would like to. And so, we try to do so by osmosis. There are always sleep timers to take advantage of, so if you find yourself living with someone like us, keep that in mind and let us do our thing.

Friendship
Non-Problems

How to Be a Friend to a Blogger

In most cases, if you are looking to make friends with a blogger, all you have to do is kiss his or her ass through a series of e-mails. (But this won't work with us.) Just as in any friendship, you'll have to appeal to the other person's ego, but you'll just have to work harder to win over the fragile blogger ego. (But not ours.) You should get your ego-massage certification well in advance. (But we have no idea how to do this.) There are mail-order programs that you can probably learn more about by e-mailing yet other people and appealing to *their* egos. (But still not ours.) Basically, your life from now on will be a series of appeals to other people's egos. (Nope, not ours.) Have fun with that. (But not us.)

Once you have secured a friendship with a blogger, get ready for more fun with ego-placating. You more or less have a responsibility to keep up with your object of friendship's public work. The only time you can get out of this is if they are behind a paywall. Otherwise, your blogger friend's work is free and there's no excuse (except for every excuse) not to be at least aware of what's going on in their professional/hobby life.

You can ignore the last paragraph if you, too, are a blogger because you already know all of this. It won't be held against you if you do not keep abreast of your fellow blogger friends' work because (a) they know how tough it can be to keep up with others' output while you're furiously churning out your own, and (b) for that reason, they probably aren't reading yours, either. If you find yourself in a lopsided situation where you are constantly bringing up their work and they never acknowledge yours, you've found yourself in a situation where you're doing a lot of extra reading that isn't necessary. Take up a new hobby, perhaps knitting or nail accessorizing, to fill the time that you used to spend trolling your friend's blog for things to talk about with said friend. If you feel bad, offer your friend a ski cap or manicure but don't explain why. Surprise ski caps and manicures are the best ski caps and manicures.

Regardless of what you are reading/cramming into the five minutes before you see your blogger friend, there are things beyond egos to contend with. Arm yourself with the knowledge that you may get written about and that things that happen when you're hanging out don't necessarily belong to you. When you hang out with a blogger, everything is on the record. Grow a thicker skin—bloggers usually inject their opinions into everything and that may include their opinions about you, things you've done, or even stuff that they don't know that you've done, and this may result in you reading their work as a commentary on your life even when it isn't. We've said it before, but this time we mean it: have fun with that.

How to Be a Friend to a Frenemy

Don't.

Why are you bothering with this drama in your life? That's not to say that you won't be put in situations where you have to get along with someone you'd rather disembowel, but why maintain the wishy-washy, namby-pamby, hoity-toity fakeness of a transparently bitchy friendship? Just be civil, something that frenemies rarely are, with their backstabbing, double-talking, eye-rolling, leave-the-room-and-they're-gagging assiness. You're better than that, and if you aren't, then we wouldn't talk to you or even pretend to like you. You'd just be an enemy. And you and everyone else would know it, bitch.

How to Be Polite About Your Friend's Shitty Taste

If the shitty taste is confined to the realm of pop culture, this is easy enough to handle: depending on your friend's level of sensitivity, talk to him or her about it. "Bad taste" is completely subjective—it could be that your friend thinks your taste is just as shitty as you think his or hers is. Taste, after all, is so much more about *why* than *what*. Someone who likes the "coolest" stuff because it's cool and they think it will impress people has no time to even develop his or her own taste because he or she is too busy worrying about other people and not busy enough worrying about pop culture. Disagreements about relatively superficial subjects can be fun and promote bonding and at the very least give you something to talk about. Agreeing to disagree can be the best thing for a friendship and the most enjoyable expression to announce because it rhymes with itself and rhyming is cool and if you think it isn't, clearly you have terrible taste in word coordination.

If a friend has shitty taste in clothing, don't meddle, but you could push him or her in a better direction by taking him or her shopping or offering light suggestions in the realm of, say, color coordination. Be honest if asked, but only to a point. Being honest to a point is the cornerstone of friendship.

If your friend has shitty taste in significant others, it poses a much bigger problem than the aforementioned surface issues. You'll probably be expected to hang out with and get along with that significant other, which makes their shitty taste your shitty problem. The good news is that if you're young enough, these things tend to correct themselves as your friend is undoubtedly on a journey of learning all about dating and how not to make the same mistakes twice. You'll probably need to ride it out while sitting on your hands and holding your tongue. Basically, your insides will play a solo game of Twister, which is no fun, but the alternative is to estrange yourself from a friend over an asshole, which is no fun and sad. As you enter your thirties, though, you're probably not going to have the time or patience to put up with jerks. In that case, push may come to shoving your friend out of your life, at least while he or she rides out this terrible relationship. But you know what? Maybe you're the terrible one for judging your friend's happiness. Not necessarily, but it's possible given the aforementioned subjectivity of taste.

Finally, if your friend has shitty taste in friends, you are shitty. Sorry! (Not that you'd accept our apology, since you're so shitty.)

How to Be Cool with Your Dealer Without Having to Be Friends with Him

Much of the territory covered here intersects with that in the entry regarding "How to Be Social with Beauticians" (page 230). Drug dealers are every bit as much a part of the service industry as beauticians are, the difference being that what drug dealers are making pretty is your mind (until, of course, it melts). You can bet that they encounter weirder and more unsavory characters than even Rich's ex-facialist Brandy does. The secondhand stories you'll acquire merely by brief and polite discussions are little nuggets in and of themselves. Pass them around a group and see how giddy everyone becomes.

This is just generally speaking. Since the drug industry isn't regulated, you're sitting on top of a slippery slope overlooking a pool of illegality. People who do illegal things for work may tend to do illegal things for play. For example, Tracie once got her ass grabbed at a drug dealer's brick and mortar (his home). Sorry, but the Better Business Bureau isn't going to give two shits about grab-assing during a marijuana pickup. Hopefully, you don't have to spend much time with this person that you're only associating with because you want something from them (drugs) and they want something from you (money). For whatever reason, things aren't always allowed to be acknowledged as that black-and-white, so there is a dance involved, especially if you are a repeat customer and the exchanging environment is laid-back (your apartment, for example).

We've had our share of less-than-ideal run-ins with dealers (any drug deal that *doesn't* involve Rich getting his ass grabbed is less than ideal for him). Here are our stories.

When Tracie was making a purchase at one dealer's home, he and his girlfriend tried to engage Tracie and her boyfriend in group sex. It was very awkward and Tracie and her boyfriend promptly left, drugs in hand. She never used that dealer again. If you encounter a similar situation and you continue to use that dealer, you have much bigger problems than dealing with your dealer. You need to deal with your demons, fool.

One time a dealer came into Tracie's apartment on taco night and she politely but jokingly offered him a taco. He accepted and watched the remaining duration of *The Simpsons* while Tracie and her friend exchanged awkward looks over tortilla envelopes filled with beef. It actually ended up being very pleasant, but not something she'd want to do again, and it was her fault for offering him a taco. Take note and don't offer Mexican food to your dealer if you don't actually want him to stick around and eat it.

One time, Rich went to North Philadelphia with some friends to buy some street weed, which proved to be a horrible mistake when a child came up to the car, took their money, and never came back with the drugs. On the upside, when they visited a gas station ATM to get more money for weed, he and his friends were confronted by a woman in the parking lot who walked up to the car and asked them the now-immortal (in Rich's head, at any rate) question: "Got any spare pants?" Rich and his friends did not. They did, though, make their way out of Philadelphia with a few dime bags of terrible weed.

One time, Rich and a friend went driving aimlessly around Atlantic City, figuring there had to be some marijuana somewhere. They left empty bonged, but not before a stranger reached his head into Rich's friend's car and licked the friend's face after they asked him, "Do you know where we could get weed?" They promptly drove away because obviously he did not, and what he was dealing (saliva) they were not buying.

One time, Tracie's former dealer made her listen to his rap single in the car and she had to wait until the song was over to get her drugs. She politely complimented his flow and then added a compliment about his Looney Tunes jeans. When she gave him the money, which happened to be mostly singles, he asked her if she was a dancer. She said, "No."

A good rule of thumb is that the harder the drugs you're buying, the harder the dealer is. Proceed with caution.

How to Be a Good Pet Owner

Do: Love your pet.
Don't: Make love to your pet.

Do: Take your pet on vacations.
Don't: Give your pet a Sex on the Beach (also don't have sex on the beach with your pet, or anywhere else for that matter).

Do: Take your pet to the beach, if they're into it and it's allowed.
Don't: Buy your pet a bathing suit.

Do: Get your pet's coat groomed as needed.
Don't: Get your pet a weave.

Do: Cut your pet's nails.
Don't: Paint your pet's nails.

Do: Sing "Party All the Time" to your pet by replacing your pet's species for the word *girl* in that song (e.g., "My chinchilla wants to party all the time, party all the time, party all the time").
Don't: Take your pet to parties and allow him or her to roam freely, at the mercy of the unstable legs of drunk people (*especially* if it's a chinchilla).

Do: Talk to your pet.
Don't: Talk down to your pet, unless your pet is on the ground, which it probably is.

Do: Clothe your pet, as the weather calls for it.
Don't: Include bondage gear in that clothing.

Do: Take time to research a diet tailored to your pet's breed.

Don't: Feed your pet Doritos and Pepsi. Pets are not Federline children.

Do: Play with your pet.

Don't: Play with yourself in front of your pet (although, if your pet is free-roaming, some overlap is inevitable and will hopefully not scar your pet emotionally).

Do: Bathe your pet.

Don't: Bathe with your pet.

Do: Clean up your pet's waste.

Don't: Smear yourself with it.

Do: Things to relax your pet, including but not limited to massage.

Don't: Include giving them cigarettes on that list.

Do: Feed your pet.

Don't: Take your pet to a restaurant.

Do: Give your pet a middle name.

Don't: Give your pet a confirmation name.

Do: Give your pet holiday presents.

Don't: Get your pet baptized.

Do: Let your pet sleep with you.

Don't: Let your pet on the bed while you're having sex.

Do: Brag about your pet to others, animal lovers or not.

Don't: Ignore the fact that everyone else feels the same damn way about their pet (more or less) and your animal is only as special as your words make it. Unless your animal really is "special" (and by that, we mean developmentally disabled).

Do: Allow your pet to watch television.
Don't: Leave the TV on Cinemax, especially at night.

Do: Get your pet wet when necessary.
Don't: Feed your pet after midnight.

How to Be Aware Your Pet Is Gay

It can be difficult to tell if your pet is gay, because with all that fur, you can't always determine the sex of what they're mounting or being mounted by. Maybe even they can't tell sometimes. Alternatively, maybe your pet is a bottom, or maybe it's just lazy.

Is your pet a bonobo monkey? If so, he or she is at least bisexual. Sometimes people and animals are so horny, they'll take whatever they can get. Such is the case with bonobos, who engage in sexual contact whenever something happens, such as a box being thrown at them. Literally.

Is your pet a penguin? If so, do you live in Antarctica? (And if so, do *you* even have sex? Or do you masturbate all the time because no one else lives there? Just curious.) Anyhow, if your pet is a penguin and he is named Roy or Silo, congratulations. You are the owner of a famously gay (or ex-gay) penguin. But seriously, boy penguins enjoy nesting with each other, so keep an eye on the penis-havers.

Is your pet a mallard? Mallards are typically symbols of Middle America's decorative masculinity (as seen in studies, on belt buckles, and in the *Jersey Shore* house), but little do the probable homophobes know that these ducks like dicks. Male mallards (or, as we like to call them, *maleards*) ditch their duckling mamas once the eggs hatch. They're strictly duckly when not begrudgingly fertilizing female eggs.

Is your pet a greylag goose? Greylag geese groups often are disproportionately male, and so, because it's better to be gay than lonely, dude geese will pair up.

Is your pet a giraffe? They'll neck with anyone. Watch out.

Is your pet a western gull? Gull society is structured so that being part of a couple, any couple, is better for a gull's social standing than bachelorhood. So they'll do dudes just to save face (which makes them radical compared to humans). Also, both males and females deep-throat extremely well.

Is your pet a dog? If so, and if it's a boy dog, he may enjoy sniffing balls. That is normal, but also gay. If it's a girl dog, rely on your groomer: if she comes back with a kerchief around her neck instead of a bow in her hair, that groomer saw something in that bitch that was butch. Sometimes you have to rely on other people to tell you about your pets because other people, unlike your pets, can talk.

Is your pet a cat? If it's a boy cat, try petting his lower back gently. If he arches up his back and presents his butthole, he probably wants to be rammed. That's so weird. Why does he do that? Because he is gay. If it's a girl cat and you are a girl, you made her gay, like it or not. If you are single, she's very gay.

Is your pet a gerbil? If so, all it takes to get him or her to have same-sex contact is a tube and a human butthole. We hear this is what turned out the hamsters of a certain A-list actor and Philadelphia-area newscaster.

Is your pet a turtle? It doesn't even matter if he or she is gay, because turtle sex is the funniest in the animal kingdom. (Go YouTube it!) Turtles may not be queer, but they sure are weird.

Is your pet a bedbug? Ew. They are known to engage in homosexual behavior, so double ew.

How to Be Around Someone You've Previously Met When You Can't Remember His or Her Name

Usually when you're faced with a situation like this, you can get around actually using the person's name in a conversation. The real bitch is when you are with a friend and you have to introduce him or her to this acquaintance. The easiest way around this is to say, "This is so and so...," referring to the person you are with—whose name you *do* know—the hope being that the acquaintance will step up to the plate and say his or her own name in the introduction. And you know what? If that person doesn't, then he or she is a stupid idiot who can't pick up on social cues and thus probably won't even realize that you are making your own social faux pas. So whatever.

Otherwise, if you're just having a normal conversation and, say, weren't properly introduced or have forgotten the person's name over the course of that conversation, you can use blanket terms of endearment for statements that require some kind of name. This may make you come off as eccentric, but it's much more embarrassing to call someone by the wrong name than a stupid blanket term. Depending on the person, you can refer to him or her as:

- Blanket
- Blanket Jackson
- Prince
- Paris
- Dude
- Homey
- Sweetie
- Hun
- Sugar
- Baby
- Girl
- Baby girl
- Boy
- Baby boy

- Son
- Baby mama
- Girlfriend
- Mami
- Papi
- Ma
- Pa
- Mommy
- Daddy
- Nephew
- Cousin
- Cuz
- Brother
- Bro
- Baby bro
- Brah
- Bra
- Sister
- Sis
- Sissy
- Spacek

People tangle their egos up in their names and are wounded when we forget them. For that reason, only use them when you are absolutely sure that you know them. Names, like audible farts and nose picking, are best avoided in public.

How to Be Aloof on Facebook

You need to be as uninvolved as possible. Duh. That is what being aloof is all about. The first thing you need to do is disable the chat feature, so people won't be able to tell that you are online. The next thing to do is be arbitrary about what you "like." This means liking a friend's status update about passing a test or a Lil B video (or whatever the kids are listening to these days) and not liking a friend's wedding photos or video footage of your niece (if she is in the tub, this will not only make you look aloof, but also like you have no interest in pedophilia—two birds with no thumbs-up). Basically, tailor your perceived interests to have no rhyme or reason. The irony is that you are putting tons of work then into seeming aloof, but here we'll debunk a myth: what's outside is far more important than what's inside. If people think you are aloof, that's better than actually being aloof. After all, you don't get to write your own obituary, and if you want it to note your aloofness, you need to get to work.

Accept friend requests but never make them. Let them sit for a while, as though you couldn't possibly be bothered to check (even if you have been actually very up on your Facebooking). This is a good rule to apply to real life as well: nothing says cool like refusing to chase down friends. Let them come to you, and if no one does, at least you know that no one's paying enough attention to care anyway.

How to Be Gay-Friendly

If you are straight and want to be a friend of friends of Dorothy, your motto from now on, instead of "No homo," is "Yes, homo." If you're not going to be opening your ass, the least you can do is open your mind. A great way to be gay-friendly, then, is to do some quick research on the history of gay people, specifically in America. Watch *Stonewall Uprising* or *Personal Best*, or listen to some disco or Ani DiFranco. A little bit of knowledge on your part will show that you care, although you can always ask questions and any reasonable gay person will tell you all about his or her life and probably do a nice job of contrasting it to yours. Don't count on always running into *Dancer from the Dance*–quoting expert queers, but do count on being educated by their life experiences.

Just as in any friendship, common ground provides a fantastic inroad to bonding. While discussing and dissecting difference is so much fun, provided that everyone keeps their heads about them (and/ or in their pants, depending on the head), finding points of similarity can be just as rewarding. Duh, you know this because you are at least a reasonably functioning social creature, but you might even be surprised where such convergences can occur. Rich has had plenty of conversations with straight men (and women, for that matter) about sex that have revealed similar attitudes and even practices, regardless of the particular parts involved. When you get down to it, in this particular case, the difference is about as deep as a butthole and/or vagina—which is to say, not very deep at all. If the idea of your straight ass discussing sex with a gay person disgusts you, you aren't working hard enough.

Being friends with gay people doesn't just mean that you will have accessories to show off like new sneakers or a handbag. Gay people will not fit in your purse like a Yorkie, no matter how hard you attempt to squeeze them in it or how much they adore it. Being gay-friendly does not mean that you now have an outrageous shopping companion, nor do you have a free get-out-of-homophobia card. (If you have to say, "I have gay friends," you probably just did something that means you're not holding up your end of the bargain.)

The bottom line at the end of the day is that if you're interested in being gay-friendly, then you're already accepting gay people as people. Thus, the simplest way to be gay-friendly is to be friendly, period.

How to Be Free of Bullshit Obligations

A wise man—or maybe it was a hooker who worked on a cash-only basis—once said, "Don't write a check with your mouth that your ass can't cash." We agree with that man or whore (and many other whores, for that matter). What the problem of bullshit obligations comes down to is other people infiltrating your psyche and weighing you down with a sense of guilt, and frankly, you not being strong enough to push back. To refer to another famous quote, "No one can make you feel inferior without your consent," and we think the same is true for obligation. The only problem is that a hooker didn't say this; Eleanor Roosevelt did. We think she was okay, but we trust hookers more.

In order to be free of the bullshit obligations that life saddles you with, you have to make like Fantasia Barrino and free yourself. This means, somewhat unfortunately, sometimes not making a show of anything you do because you don't want people to get the idea that you do things. Like we told you in "How to Be Late All the Time Without People Hating You" (page 70), the key to an easy life is to keep others' expectations of you as low as possible. We're all graded on a curve, and overachievers not only suffer because of all the achieving they must do, but because their failures seem like a much bigger deal in light of said achievements.

Don't set a standard for yourself as being the kind of person who picks people up from airports or helps a friend who's too cheap to hire movers transport his or her life from one apartment to the next. Because you won't cross people's minds to call on when these things come up, you won't be in people's minds to be resented when you don't deliver.

We're advocating this in the name of self-preservation: you need time to do your own shit, and you'll find that most of the time when you go out of your way to help people, they will not respond with proper appreciation, nor will they reciprocate the favor down the road. And then you will be left with your own anger.

Of course, if you are in the honorable and miniscule segment of the population that *truly* enjoys doing things for other people, by all means go ahead. We have some dry-cleaning and dry-walling and dry-humping that need to be accomplished and will gladly call on you for your services.

(But in the case of the dry-humping, only if you're hot.)

How to Be When Your Friend Has a Miscarriage

Do: Put your head on her shoulder and offer consolation.

Don't: Laugh...unless it is, in effect, a freebie abortion. Then you can both laugh and high-five and go out to dinner that night with money that would have otherwise been sucked up/out by a doctor.

How to Be Sociable
Among Strangers

The key to sociability is prep work. Watch the news (*Entertainment Tonight* counts), a movie, a sporting event if you must—anything current that could provide a topic of conversation. There's nothing worse than being around a bunch of people and having nothing to say. The I'm-a-good-listener act works for only so long. In the best-case scenario, people will keep you around to talk at you and not with you. You are not anyone's set of hired ears, but if you are, you'd better be getting paid (which you will not be).

When introducing topics, be specific. Just because few people your age are among the 10 million Americans who tune in each day to watch the adventures and rantings of Judge Judith Sheindlin does not mean that you will not find another fellow minority among the crowd. If you do, you'll know it's a match. If you don't, you can school people on a subject they know far too little about. And if they don't like that, they aren't anyone you'd want to be friends with anyway. In fact, *Judge Judy* is a terrific topic for screening out assholes, bores, and people lacking simple common sense.

Now, we understand that not all shyness can be overcome with pop culture savvy. This is where booze comes in. You don't need us to tell you that alcohol is a social lubricant, but we will anyway because *lubricant* is a sexual word and we like it. Drink. Go now. When meeting strangers for the first time, however, avoid pot (unless they offer it to you, in which case you don't want to come off as a square, so you must smoke even if you normally don't). Getting stoned will make you awkward and will make everything seem weird, including you. Understand that probably everyone else feels that way, unless they're all friends already. In that case, they are probably getting you high just to fuck with you. Sorry to make you more paranoid than you already will be, but that's what it is.

So what it boils down to is: get drunk and talk about *Judge Judy*. Even if you do this by yourself, you'll still be entertained.

How to Be Able to Bring Drugs to a Party and Get Fucked Up Without Giving Them All Away or Looking Like a Selfish Asshole

How *do* you do this?

(We're not including cocaine, which has its own culture of secrecy that is perfect for situations like this but is probably bad for you in general, when you consider so many of our fallen stars. Do you sing? You'll ruin your voice with that shit.)

While we think that this is a problem with no solution—and that there is at least one asshole in any given situation—we're open to suggestions, so e-mail us at partyanimals@potpsychology.com.

Body and Diet
Non-Problems

How to Be Pregnant

Take advantage of people's kindness during this part of your life, because the world is a cruel place but one that for some reason likes pregnant women. Take seats on the subway that are offered to you. Allow others to hold your heavy bags. Accept back massages from people you trust. Take the elevator instead of the stairs to the second floor. Demand door-to-door service regardless of distance.

Take advantage of not having to worry about your waistline. This is your chance to eat lard. By the stick. Fuck a salad unless it's drenched in cream. You're going to lose all the weight when you breast-feed anyway (you *are* going to breast-feed, right? Right?), and this is the first time since childhood when you can eat without remorse or using your brain at all. Your child will soon do this, and then when you get jealous of him or her, at least you won't be thinking back to the halcyon days of your childhood; you'll be reminded of that time a few years ago when your ankles were swollen and you were hot and uncomfortable all the time and used food as a coping device.

Refrain from taking naked pregnant pictures, unless you're a celebrity. Gotta get those mag covers! Otherwise, you're just a weirdo who thinks they're a celebrity, and news flash: no one's putting your pregnant ass on any magazine cover anytime soon. Who do you even share that shit with? Your kids will be grossed out and, to be honest, so will everyone else with any sense. Avoid, avoid, avoid.

Tracie's doctor also said, "Don't be an alcoholic," which is a very duuuuhh statement, and it's also easier said than done. If that were so easy, the very concept of rehab wouldn't exist. But yeah, don't drink or do drugs or smoke when you're leasing a womb. Because then you are going to have to deal with that and a little bit of pregnancy pleasure could lead to years and years of a screaming brat. At least give your kid a shot in life.

All of this is to say, put down whatever you're smoking and read a different book if you're pregnant. Stoned people have no idea what to do with a fetus, and apparently, neither do you. Get help.

Also, if you read this entry in the hopes of learning how to get pregnant, the answer is simple: place a penis inside of your vagina and move around until it ejaculates. Repeat as necessary.

How to Be Okay with Your Abortion

The biggest tip is: don't be precious about it. The second biggest tip is: don't be Precious-Based-on-the-Novel-*Push*-by-Sapphire about it (which means not having one so that you have to raise your kids with HIV as you attempt to get your GED).

Really, what a lot of pro-lifers don't understand is that women usually are okay with their abortions. The people who aren't okay with an embryo being aborted are those who aren't pregnant. It's societal interference that's the biggest burden on women who are getting them. It's the nuts on picket lines and the old ladies with past-prime uteruses and virgins and the fucking men—all people who have no chance of having to be put in a situation where they have to make a choice—who are the ones who want to take the choice away and shame those who've exercised that choice. Fuck all that noise, but don't do it without a condom or you could get pregnant again.

How to Be Around and About Vaginas When You're a Gay Man

If you are a gay man in the company of exposed female genitalia, you first need to reconsider your lifestyle choice. We are not saying being gay is a lifestyle or even a choice, but being around pussy is. If you don't like cats, stay out of their box, whether it's of the litter or lady-loins variety. This is generally speaking—sometimes being around a whisker biscuit is unavoidable. There is a certain type of woman who may think showing you her naked crotch is funny or even just a normal thing to do. Also, maybe you're a stylist or some kind of fashion hanger-on who finds himself backstage at fashion shows. Are there such things as male waxers? We don't know, but if you are one, we feel your pain. It feels like hair being ripped out of us.

So let's just say that you aren't being a weirdo or self-administering exposure therapy to convert, and that your keeping company with vaginas is simply accidental. Be respectful, regardless. Don't make faces at vaginas you don't intend on putting your face on. Don't poke at them. Keep away your penis and your pens. Don't hold your nose and say, "Who opened a can of tuna?" Don't say "Ew" out loud, even if you're thinking it in your head. Don't compliment her on the size of her clit. She'll get the wrong idea. Don't hold your cigarette too close. It's probably not flammable, but we haven't tested every vagina to make sure yet, so it's better to be safe than fanning a flaming fanny. Your friend who is exposing herself to you may not know what class is, but that doesn't mean *you* have to abandon it.

But even if you never find yourself on a first-name, face-to-face basis with Scarlett O'Hairy, please conduct yourself with utmost respect. This goes for when referring to female genitalia, even if you're out of ear-/hole-shot. We know you don't like pussy. It's okay. One man's unwanted snatch is another man's pleasure. That is implicit in the existence of homosexuality, and to go on at any length about how "disgusting" vaginas are is redundant. Go find a cock to occupy your time. Everyone will be happier, especially you because you are gay. In the words of Rich's middle-school home economics teacher Mrs. Crist, who mysteriously developed an extremely bloodshot eye overnight and was the subject of ridicule among her students the next day: if you don't like it, don't look at it. And certainly don't fuck it, because it doesn't want you anyway.

The next time you want to say something rotten about vaginas, just remember you came from one.

How to Be the Owner of an Uncircumcised Penis

Clean it. If we wanted cheese, we'd go to Simply Fondue.

How to Be Attractive
in the Pubic Area

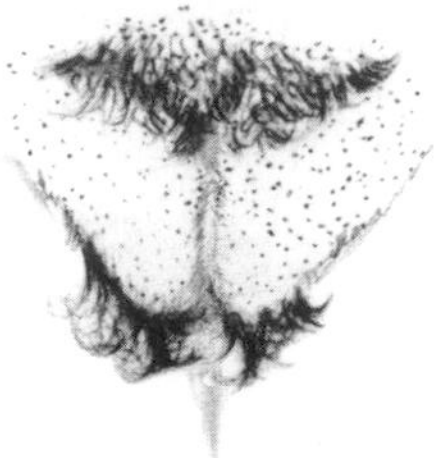

MULLET

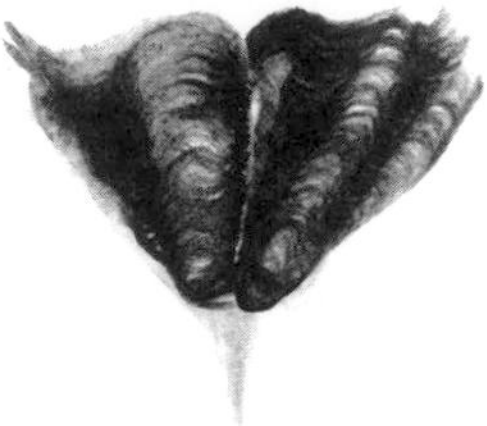

GIBSON GIRL

FINGER WAVES

DREADLOCKS

PIPPI LONGSTOCKING

MC LYTE

KID FROM KID-N-PLAY

CORNROWS

By Elizabeth Carey Smith

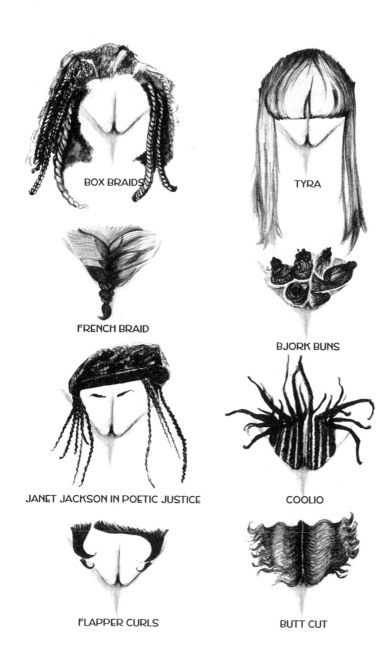

BOX BRAIDS

TYRA

FRENCH BRAID

BJORK BUNS

JANET JACKSON IN POETIC JUSTICE

COOLIO

FLAPPER CURLS

BUTT CUT

How to Be Covert When Scratching Your Crotch

In the event of crotch itch, the ideal strategy is to put your hand down your pants and dig in. Depending on your surroundings, this may not be possible to do without making enemies or provoking gossip. If you want to be the Crotch Guy because you're a pervert, you probably know more ways than we do to attain that reputation. If you don't want to be that guy/girl, you're going to have to obscure your itch sitch.

If your clothes are tight enough, you may get away with grinding up against them by swiveling your hips. Adding a shimmy to your walk can make all the difference. If you are seated, cross your legs—*hard*. You can attempt to make a rubbing motion with your legs, but if you are wearing corduroys, watch out, because you will catch on fire. And that will make your crotch infinitely itchier. For an advanced technique, try crossing your legs tightly, turning your body in the process. Land your elbow in your crotch for a satisfying compromise.

If you're certain that eyes will be on you, trying scratching your thigh, and as you pull your arm up, graze your crotch. If you repeat this a couple hundred times, you may find relief at last.

If you're so concerned and plagued by this problem, why not just go to the bathroom or an abandoned stairwell and itch to your crotch's content? If that is impossible and none of these solutions work, just go for it and don't look anyone in the eye. If you don't know them, it doesn't matter anyway.

How to Be About Your Areola Hair

One in six women have areola hair. Usually, they're long, dark strays, but however few, they're still gross. The best thing to do is to pluck them...unless you're seeing someone who's into boob hair. In that case, a hair on your tit is a feather in your cap. But seriously, if you have what looks like a John Waters mustache surrounding your nipple, then you might have something called polycystic ovary syndrome, in which case you should put down this book and go to the doctor.

Good rule of thumb/nipple: anytime something on your body is disturbing, you probably shouldn't turn to books written by potheads but by doctors. However, if you don't have health insurance or the drive to get off your ass, smoking pot will help you forget about everything that's wrong with you. Maybe. It could also make you dwell on it. A better rule of thumb/nipple: avoid mirrors when high.

As for the men, your areola hair is fine. Sorry, ladies, that's just how the world works. We didn't make it, but we also don't feel like looking at tit hair in it.

And by the way, if you think we're judging bodies unfairly, we're not only the nipple hair presidents, we're also clients. Both of us have nipple hair, and while Rich has never once given his any thought, Tracie has photographed hers and compared it to currency.

Evidence below:

What we are trying to say is that you are not alone. We are here with you and Lisa Marie Presley, who's draped naked (and hairless) across us as we sit amongst marble pillars.

How to Be Hemorrhoidal

If you actually want to have hemorrhoids, you are a weirdo beyond help in most cases except for this one because we can actually help you get them. You're asking us because we know about these things. Follow these steps for a flaming anus and/or fire in the hole:

1. Eat a lot of foods that will create blockage in your bowels. These include but are not limited to: various cheeses (particularly Velveeta, which is processed to the point of interfering with your process), abundant portions of fatty meats, all types of candy, snacks (basically, any kind of high-fat or high-sugar/low-fiber concoction), cotton, wet cement, and Play-Doh.

2. If you followed step 1 correctly, you've created a blockage the size and consistency of a bocce ball. Now it's time to push! But don't do that without getting on the toilet first. Actually, you're probably already there if you're reading this book. Push hard! Harder! Harder still! Bear down! Hold your breath and don't stop pushing until you feel as though you'll burst a blood vessel in your face. Think about something that makes you very angry. Don't stop until you get that poop out. Set aside hours if you must. Cancel plans from the toilet. Tell people "I'm washing my hair" and then, since you have the time and are in the bathroom anyway, wash your hair.

3. Now that you've successfully voided your bowels, turn around to look at your dirty work. If you've followed our advice, in plain view will be what we call a Daniel Day-Lewis. In other words, there will be blood. Ideally, when you go to wipe, it will hurt. We should once again remind you that this is *your* ideal, not ours. We don't want hemorrhoids, you freak. If you cannot sit down comfortably for the next twenty minutes, congratulations. You're now in the running to have America's next top hemorrhoid.

(While you're bearing down, also bear in mind that food is arguably the most enjoyable way to get hemorrhoids, but it is not the only way. Another arguably enjoyable way is anal sex. Make sure to go light on the lube and heavy on the thrusting for optimal results. Other methods include sitting on your asshole for twelve hours at a time for several days in a row, chronic diarrhea, obesity, or pregnancy. There are also vaginal hemorrhoids, but we feel the less said about them, the better. If you're really interested in getting them, consult a doctor and make sure his or her concentration is psychiatry.)

Now, if you are more reasonable in your interests and are merely seeking how to live with hemorrhoids that you never wanted in the first place, listen up: the best source of relief are Tucks Medicated Pads. They are not paying us to write this, but we wish they were, and if they would like to, we'll gladly devote our next book solely to our love of Tucks Medicated Pads. Perhaps we can come up with new uses for them much like the rash of T-shirt-transformation books that broke out about a decade ago. We suspect, for example, that they'd make good pasties and we're willing to test that out if the price is right.

You can mess around (but don't make an actual mess because you're gross enough down there) with creams and ointments, but disposable pads like those made by Tucks are probably the most sanitary solution. Inflatable donut seats may feel good at the moment, but they'll only prolong your condition. Al Bundy had a 'roids pillow, and the last thing you need when you're dealing with hemorrhoids is comparisons to people on *Married...with Children*, as much of an American treasure as Kelly Bundy was.

How to Be a Pothead
Without Gaining Weight

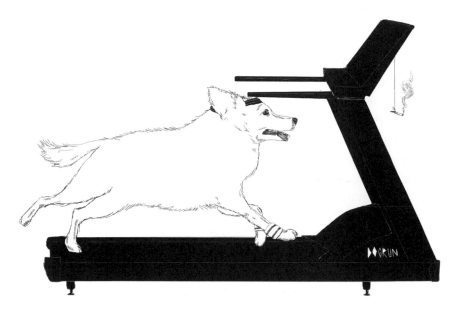

Pot is said to speed up your metabolism. We cannot confirm or deny this because we are not scientists and are too lazy to look it up. Assuming this *is* true, you can actually lose weight from marijuana use if you can control yourself. However, you won't be able to because you will be on drugs. That's the whole point.

The key to not eating like a dog with opposable thumbs is to prepare your snacks in advance of getting high. If you buy a crate of blueberries, you will eat that crate, but at least you won't be eating a crate of donuts. Or dipping Milano cookies into peanut butter. Or toasting taco shells, breaking them up, and making nachos out of them. Or eating ramen noodles raw. Or making S'mores and substituting Cool Whip for marshmallows. Or eating a whole bag of marshmallows in one mouthful. That's dangerous and best reserved for kids on YouTube. Only idiots would put their marijuana-fueled exploits online.

Really, you could just do whatever and then attempt to exercise it away, but keep in mind that exercise has only a 25 percent effect on your weight, with food providing the other 75 percent, or so we read once, we think. We cannot confirm or deny this, either, for the same reasons as above, which we are now too lazy to retype.

If you want to be a pothead without gaining weight, try not to be this lazy. Do as we say, not as we do.

How to Be a Marijuana User with Clean Urine

Note to yourself: The following information is based on personal experience and not medical expertise. Duh. Like all of our advice, it's on you if you decide to follow it. We'd probably advise against it. Also, keep in mind that this worked thirteen years ago. We know nothing of the advances in drug-testing technology. Oh yeah, also keep in mind that drugs are illegal and cheating is bad, even if the test you're cheating on is just a stupid drug test.

Perhaps you've found yourself in a situation where you have to take a drug test. And perhaps you are a marijuana enthusiast or just partake in the pleasure sporadically. This intersection is not good, but we have some tips on how you can pass a urine test, and piss like you're off the pot.

The problem—well, one problem—with employee drug test screening is that urine tests can detect traces of marijuana for up to six weeks. And because they detect nonactive metabolites instead of the psychoactive ingredient in marijuana, the tests don't actually measure impairment, but just call out recreational weed smokers. It's like getting busted for getting drunk three Saturdays ago. Typically, large companies will spring drug screening on new hires, giving them very little time to prepare and certainly not enough time for any drugs to pass out of their systems naturally.

1. **Don't bother with commercial urine cleansers.** You might have seen them advertised in stoner mags, but there is no real scientific evidence that urine cleansers are effective. They can be pricey (ranging from $20 to $50), mostly because their manufacturers are preying on people who are freaking out about possibly losing their jobs. But if you read the ingredients, they usually contain herbal diuretics like goldenseal that can easily be purchased at the drugstore for half the cash (and that probably don't even work anyhow). Plus, because most

urine cleansers instruct you to chug the drink about an hour before your test, you're really gambling by trusting that your metabolism operates at the same rate as that of the company's control group.

2. **Drink water.** Drink lots and lots and lots of water—gallons of it—from the time you learn about your test up until the big moment. While you can't realistically detoxify your body of all signs of marijuana use in a short period of time, you can temporarily do so, in your urine anyway, by flushing your system. Water is your best bet, best weapon, and best friend when it comes to passing a piss test.

3. **Take Midol.** You can increase your pee flow by taking diuretics. Coffee and cranberry juice can be a little too weak, and you want to stay away from diet pills (which are also diuretics) because there's always a chance that you could actually test positive for some kind of amphetamine. Some folks suggest taking 80 milligrams of the prescription drug Lasix (which is used to treat high blood pressure), but good luck getting your hands on that. Stick with PMS medication used to treat bloating, like Midol. It's safer and more readily available.

4. **Take a B-complex multivitamin.** Between drinking all the fluids and taking the diuretics, your urine will probably be pretty watered down and almost clear. This can raise suspicions for some lab technicians. B_2 or B_{12} can help to bring back that yellow glow, so take 100 milligrams of a B-complex multivitamin two hours before your test.

5. **Take aspirin.** Studies indicate that aspirin interferes with EMIT (enzyme multiplied immunoassay technique) drug screening, masking certain parts of the spectrum that urine testing checks. Take four aspirin four to six hours before your test.

6. **Timing is everything.** You'll want to give your best (cleanest) sample of urine—time of day and time of stream play into your

success with this. You'll want to pee at least twice before your test. (Your first pee of the day tends to be the "dirtiest.") When you're actually taking the test, catch your urine in the cup mid-stream. Let a little flow before aiming at the cup, and take it away before you're done peeing.

Good luck!

How to Be Gassy in Public

If you have a problem with farting in public, what you *don't* want to do is go to a bookstore, because that is almost guaranteed to give you gas. Have you ever noticed that in your lifetime of buying books? Perhaps it is the smell of book glue and dust jackets, or the fact that it's so quiet in there, but bookstores are notorious for creating a psychosomatic need to pass gas. Thankfully, electronic books have helped with this situation. (Once again, technological advances save the day!) But if a trip to the bookstore is unavoidable, and you are met with the urge to fart, then go to the children's section, because kids are like farts: they're loud and they stink. You'll be right at home.

But let's get out of the bookstore. You already have a book in your hand. You probably have plenty of others at home you haven't read yet.

The key to being gassy in public—meaning how to do it without being embarrassed or "caught"—is to keep it quiet and keep it moving. If you're old enough to know how to read, then surely by now you must have acquired the ability to change a fart from an audible one to a quiet one. (It's hard to really spell out the specifics of this process, but you totally know what we mean, so don't act like you don't.) And here's a tip: you can help the process along by sticking your hands in your back pockets and manually spreading your butt cheeks to minimize sound.

But your best bet is to stay mobile. This means: fart while walking briskly on the street, moving from one room into another at a party, or boarding a plane. Actually, airplane farting is ideal. The engines are so loud that you can literally have a conversation with the stranger sitting next to you while you practically propel the plane with your own ass.

Or just grow old. Because the older you get, the less you care about this kind of shit. It's actually liberating, as well as totally disgusting. Your colon will thank you.

How to Be Around Fireworks

We know someone who lost his eye because he was at a Fourth of July party with drunk idiots who were illegally setting off fireworks, one of which went into his face. Our advice to you is to stay away from drunk people with fireworks. Only look at fireworks from afar when they're part of a legally sanctioned display. Even though we didn't stick around for them when we visited together a few years ago, we recommend Disney World's.

What goes without saying here, though we're about to say it, is that the way to be around fireworks is amazed and agog while keeping your distance. We can't say that enough. Keep your distance.

Keep your distance.

Keep your distance.

We also recommend you keeping your distance from Katy Perry when possible. Baby, you're not a firework because if you were then you'd be on fire or would have already exploded. You'd be worse off than a primordial dwarf, who typically has a very short lifespan (about thirty years max). We don't mean offense to primordial dwarves. We actually like them a lot and wish they'd stick around longer.

How to Be Open with Your Hairdresser About a Bad Haircut

This is very difficult. You don't want to offend this person, because your look is in their hands. And also in their hands is a pair of scissors that could be in your neck with a single swipe. At the same time, you want to get what you paid for, and if you're getting a decent haircut, you're *paying* for it. It might seem silly and immature, but if crying is your honest response when looking in the mirror, don't hide your tears. (A decade's worth of *America's Next Top Model* should have made that much obvious.) Your hairdresser will respond sympathetically, unless he or she is a robot. In that case, your hairdresser is probably a Flowbee, and it's your own fault that your hair looks bad.

There's no reason for you to be rude unless the hairdresser introduces rudeness. The fact that artistry factors into a hairdresser's job can complicate things, but just remember: your hairdresser is in the service industry. He or she works for tips, and as anyone who works for tips understands, the customer is always right. And if he or she is playing the artistry card, last we checked, Picasso didn't have a tip jar next to his easel (and rest assured, we did check and it's nowhere to be found in the top seven entries on Google using the search term *Picasso tip jar*).

If your hairdresser is offended by your reaction to your haircut, you're probably part of a journey that will lead him or her to being less offended when issues like this come up in the future. Again, if your hairdresser is a Flowbee, this doesn't apply, since Flowbees can't learn.

And besides, you can always just go to a new hairdresser or wait for it to grow out. You aren't Barbie. This damage is not irreparable. Use this time of bad hair to get into hats, weaves, wigs, and extensions. Every girl needs that period.

(Note: As we were writing this entry, we could not stop singing Lucille Cataldo's "Hairdresser," from the early '80s public access talent show *Stairway to Stardom*. If you are unfamiliar with this gorgeous composition, we recommend you drop everything [even if you're reading this on an iPad—drop it!] and watch it now. Understanding the genius of this song is the key to understanding the people that we are today.)

How to Be Social with Beauticians

Sometimes, the answer to this one is easy: don't. Some procedures don't require conversation or niceties and, in fact, such chatter could make them even more awkward. Some qualifying instances include a facial mask treatment or a pedicure, which finds your worker far enough from you to make conversation more effort than it should be. Your procedure should be relaxing, not taxing.

That said, receiving beauty treatments like facials, haircuts, or manicures brings you into close proximity with another human being, and conversation feels only natural. If you feel like verbalizing anything that goes through your head, by all means, do it. At the same time, there is no obligation for you to say anything. The onus is on the esthetician to introduce a topic and keep it moving. After all, he or she is in the service industry, and small talk is an implied part of his or her job description.

If you don't want to reveal too much about yourself, don't. Any beautician worth his or her salt will take over and chatter the time away. Before discovering the miracle drug that is Retinol, Rich used to get facials regularly with an Ecuadorian woman named Brandy, who'd play top forty music when he came in (changing over from the new age shit they usually play to soothe people) and talk at length about her daughter, whom she sometimes had custody of and sometimes didn't and who may have been breast-fed and/or molested by her sixty-year-old babysitter, who had "very big titties and a wig in her hair." The casual way Brandy described her child's trauma to a virtual stranger made Rich wonder if he was hearing her right. If so, that probably made her some kind of sociopath and not the kind of person you want near your eyeballs with an extraction tool.

A few things that she absolutely certainly did say, though, were:

"You know how French people are: very chic."

"I gave him a strong look."

"She was very husky."

"Lesbians have a lot of butterfly tattoos."

"You can't be a doctor, only a nurse." (This was in response to a zit Rich attempted to tackle himself. Of course, Brandy couldn't be a doctor either, but she was the one with access to all of the pseudomedical tools, so she was the doctor in this situation.)

Brandy also confirmed the long-standing rumor that one of the most beloved rappers working today has a huge penis because he apparently went in to get a facial himself and it was visible underneath the sheet they have you put on while you're getting work done.

And so, if Rich had shut out Brandy, he never would have heard any of this wonderful, helpful, troubling information, and neither would you.

Self-Improvement
Non-Problems

How to Be a Pothead
Without Being a Loser

The first thing you need is something else going on in your life. If your potheadedness leads you to your parents' basement or couch on a full-time basis, you are a loser. If you're holding down a job and getting high constantly, you are not a loser. (Unless you're operating heavy machinery—making your inebriation someone else's problem is a really losery thing to do. Pot doesn't kill people; losers kill people.)

But let's say you still feel like your marijuana use is keeping you from being all that you can be, yet you have no interest in joining the army. (Not that you could with your THC-infused piss, anyway. Or wait, could you? Do they drug test before you enter the army? We don't know and we're not going to find out because we don't care, nor are we joining the army.) Let's say you once thought your one ambition in life was to sit around and get high, but now you're having second, albeit cloudy, thoughts. The best thing you can do to turn that frown upside down into a weird weedy happy face is to harness the creative power of marijuana. Produce. We'll let you in on a little piece of Pot Psychology history: every weekend, at least on one night, we would sit around and get high and watch TV and stuff. When the idea of Pot Psychology came around, our weekends were very much the same, except instead of sitting around passively, we were creating things actively. And now look: we have a book with our names on it. That makes us officially not losers, and if you still want to call us losers, chances are you don't have a book with your name on it, unless you wrote it on with a Sharpie. You should probably get high and get a book deal or at least chill the fuck out.

Way before we had any idea that we'd be making money off of our marijuana use, we still had the feeling of satisfaction that came from creation. We've written several blog posts that were inspired or flat-out fueled by being stoned. Tracie has made a menagerie of embroidered decorative throw pillows while high. But mostly, we like to write songs. We've been doing this for years. Allow us to share some of our musical high-deas with you. These are mostly rap songs, with the exception of "MySpace Profile," which is country.

Presents

I'm horny in your presence
I wanna give you presents.

MySpace Profile

I took a picture of a picture in a picture frame
And I printed out the printout on a printer
And put that picture of a picture in a picture frame
In a picture frame

I Wanna Sniff Yo Crotch Like a Dog

When I see your ass walkin' down the street
(I wanna sniff yo crotch like a dog)
Ooh, you make my life complete
(I wanna sniff yo crotch like a dog)
Feminine smell up in the air
(I wanna sniff yo crotch like a dog)
Party people better beware
(I wanna sniff yo crotch like a dog)

Candlestick Up Yo Ass

Candlestick up yo ass
What?
You got a candlestick up yo ass
Uh-huh.
Candlestick up yo ass
What?
You got a candlestick up yo ass
Uh-huh. Uh-huh.
Yo, you just got out of jail
Now you got something funny hanging out of your tail
What can it be? is all I ask

Motherfucker got a candlestick up his ass!
Candlestick up yo ass
What?
You got a candlestick up yo ass
Uh-huh.
Candlestick up yo ass
What?
You got a candlestick up yo ass
Uh-huh. Uh-huh.

How to Be Cool

- Sunglasses
- Cigarettes
- Air-conditioning
- Leather jackets (not leather vests)
- Date someone who wears a leather jacket (but not a leather vest)
- Ceiling fans
- Put your thumbs up and go, "Aaaay!"
- Light a match with one hand
- Silly Bandz (if you are a tween living in 2010)
- Be a parent who lets their kids engage in underage drinking
- Convertibles (If you have one, give yourself two cool points for every year above thirty-five you are but stop doing math because it isn't cool.)
- Have sex
- Refer to people as "Cool" as though it is a proper noun (e.g., "Hi, Cool!")
- Swimming pools
- Icy Hot, for a few seconds
- Fall asleep in a refrigerator
- Put a Capri Sun next to your vagina (Note: does not apply to men.)
- Instead of taking your retro cues from things that happened ten years ago, take them from things that happened seven years ago
- Don't wear underwear
- Have a lot of friends on Facebook
- Never talk about the number of friends you have on Facebook
- Own a yacht (matching apparel optional)
- Keep your shoes untied
- Shoes with no socks (but not socks with no shoes)
- Wear sneakers with a tuxedo
- Go tieless
- Go shirtless
- Go shirtless, go shoeless, go in a store, and get service
- Peg pants and a swinging chain
- Backward hat
- Inside-out T-shirts
- Hypercolor
- Don't get too cold (*Cool* describes a moderate temperature.)
- Have a cell phone
- Paint designs on your toenails
- Toe rings
- Drink lots of water
- Have sex with someone in a band

240

- Do drugs with someone in a band
- Know someone in a band and take his or her musical suggestions to heart
- Waterslides
- Take a job as an ice cream worker
- Write your phone number on a bathroom stall
- Braid your entire head (if you are white)
- Braid part of your head (if you are black)
- Roll up your sleeves
- Go to art school
- Wear shorts
- Celebrate Christmas in July
- Hang out in front of the Wawa
- Understand a Wawa reference
- Tamper with church communion wafers
- Read a book inside your hymnal at church
- Befriend a chimpanzee
- Befriend a gay person (See "How to Be Gay-Friendly," page 183.)
- Get arrested for a victimless crime
- Hang out on train tracks
- Chew gum
- Pop out of a limo's sunroof
- Twist a nerd's nipple
- Consider the mall to be your "turf" (unless you are a parent)
- Wear your bookbag on one shoulder
- Wear your overalls on one shoulder
- Get bottle service at a club
- Match your single ear piercing with your sexual orientation (straight = left ear, gay = right ear, bisexual = we're not going to make you pick, since that's your whole thing)
- Walk into a party like you're walking onto a yacht
- Dip your hat strategically below one eye
- Gavotte
- Bring something to a party (wine, flowers, casserole, drugs, etc.)
- Whatever you call it when you take the bottom of your T-shirt and pull it up through the collar
- Make idle chitchat at the urinal
- Harmonize during "Happy Birthday"
- Save winter snow in your freezer and then have a snowball fight in August
- Listen to pop music unironically

- Listen to indie music ironically
- Hands up on a roller coaster
- Spit your gum out on the ground
- Scratch your balls in public
- Walk with a limp
- Strut
- If you have crutches, pretend that one is a machine gun (as a joke)
- Remain silent about your vegetarianism
- Hold in your farts
- …until you ask someone to pull your finger
- Sit with your legs open
- Sit in a chair backward
- Keep a small animal in your pocket/bra
- Use a money clip
- Wear a pinky ring
- Wear a ring above your first knuckle
- Keep a condom in your wallet (Be mindful of the expiration date.)
- Get decorative seat belt covers for your car
- Smuggle food into the movies
- Go on a shopping spree and swing your bags on the way home
- Don't do your homework
- Don't tell Mom the babysitter's dead
- Bring back bolero ties
- Drink wine with a straw
- Snort coke off a penis/penises with a straw
- Snort coke off of boobs with a $2 bill
- Do body shots (If you are a guy, do them off a girl; if you are a girl, still do them off a girl. We aren't man haters; this is just about not getting hair in your mouth.)
- Dye your pubic hair
- Light people's cigarettes for them
- At a party, flick a light switch repeatedly to create a strobe effect
- If you are a child, sit inside clothing racks at the mall
- Buy ingredients for S'mores
- Collect bones
- Collect boners
- Get into bonsai and do it right (It's hard.)
- Get into origami and do it right (It's hard.)
- Emulate the Japanese in general and do it right (It's hard.)
- Get your face painted like a cat at the fair

- Learn how to parallel-park
- Wear opera gloves with a cape
- Wear a mask when it isn't Halloween
- Wear a turtleneck when you have a hickey
- Go easy on the scarves
- Laugh at your own joke
- Learn the lyrics to an entire contemporary rap song
- Learn the lyrics to an entire old-school rap song
- Back that thang up
- Wear control-top hose
- Walk like an Egyptian
- Do the Hustle
- Baggy jeans, Tims, thug appeal
- Trench, hat, loafs
- Dimples in ya necktie
- Apple Bottoms jeans, boots with the fur
- Bamboo earrings, at least two pair
- A Fendi bag and a bad attitude
- Extensions in your hair or even a curly weave
- New Edition Bobby Brown button on your sleeve
- Gold-tooth smile
- Folding fans (see: Karl Lagerfeld)
- If you fall off the stage, legs extended and boobs up
- Advise people on coolness

How to Be Down

Whether you are like a fourteen-year-old Brandy, wanting to be down with what your object of desire is going through, or you have your eye on a culture that you are interested in co-opting like a henna-handed, kimono-wearing, voguing, girl cowboy Madonna, the answer is always: education. This doesn't mean that you have to know everything about a group that you don't necessarily belong to, but it does mean that you always need to be willing to learn. A question is infinitely better than an incorrect assumption when it comes to a discussion of otherness. (See also, "How to Be Gay-Friendly," page 183.)

Not everyone feels this way, and in fact, many young people were discouraged from such open inquisitiveness in the '90s, when the girl-friend of *The Real World: San Francisco*'s Mohammad spoiled the great decade of diversity by snapping at his roommate Cory when she asked, "Are you mixed?" Perhaps she didn't like the implication that her skin was lighter than what Cory envisioned black people's should be, but at the same time, closing off a conversation about race that's coming from genuine curiosity is such an assy thing to do. It promotes ignorance, which is at the root of not being down.

Of course, being accepted is an entirely different matter—maybe you have all the knowledge in the world, but you smell bad or your attitude is otherwise stank. In that case, you wouldn't be down if you were a dwarf with a hunchback. Also in that case, there's little any book, even ours, could do for you. In fact, you might want to lay off the books and lay in the bath instead.

Other people's responses aside, the important thing is to read, listen to music, ask questions, etc. Keep your eyes, ears, and mind open, and you'll be well on your way. An alternative is to close your mind entirely and just tell yourself that you are down. Sad as it is to say, you'll probably wind up just as self-satisfied.

How to Be Likable

Real talk: Any fake-ass bitch on a reality show will tell you about the importance of being real. Never mind that she herself is fake. Actually, do mind that because hypocrisy is something to steer clear of if you're out to be likable (Note on our own likability: See our Hypocritical Oath page xvii, and understand that like those fake-ass bitches on reality TV, we're not here to make friends.) So basically, do as they say, not as they do (which was an actual directive stated by Tyra Banks to the confused children on *America's Next Top Model*).

Below are some other balances you must strike in the great gymnastics of social interaction. They may seem confusing, but that's life. Part of being likable is learning how to separate the ice cream from the bullshit.

You should be considerate, but not too involved.

You should be smart, but not a know-it-all.

You should be affectionate, but not touchy-feely.

You should be decisive, but not set in your ways.

You should be open, but not too open, especially if you aren't wearing panties.

You should be friendly, but not too friendly, especially if you are a child walking home from school.

You should smell good, but not fill a room with your essence.

You should be an individual, but not self-consciously weird (if you say things like "I'm soooo weird!" you have gone too far).

You should be a good listener, but not catatonic.

You should be able to find humor in things, but not too loudly.

You should be a good storyteller, but not control the funny.

You should be a good cook, but not shove that or any of your prepared foods down people's throats.

You should be into cool stuff, but not be proprietary about it.

You should be clean, but not sterile.

You should be well-kept, but not be afraid to get your hands dirty.

You should be prompt, but not for parties or your own funeral. (RIP, Elizabeth Taylor.)

You should be successful, but not at the cost of true love.

You should be powerful, but not so much so you break people's hands when you shake them.

You should be flattering, but not an ass-kisser.

You should be tall, but not intimidatingly so.

You should be blond, but not bland.

You should be a shit-talker, but not about us.

You should be civically responsible, but not a politician.

You should be fun at a party, but not throwing up.

You should be articulate, but not a grammar-police officer.

You should be big-dicked, but not unfuckable.

You should be tight-vagina'd, but not unfuckable.

You should be a good kisser, but not chokey with your tongue.

You should be naked during a one-night stand, but not emotionally.

You should be able to commiserate, but not sound whiny.

You should offer to pick up the check, but not if it's just an excuse to show off your wealth.

You should be an animal lover, but not like *that*.

How to Be Sophisticated Without Being Snobby

Snobbery is just insecurity with its nose turned up. It's acting out as a result of being uncomfortable and unsure of oneself. It's the hoity-toity cousin of nastiness, and everyone knows nasty people hate themselves the most.

Whereas snobbery comes from hating oneself, sophistication comes from knowing oneself. Not to get too self-helpy on you (even though getting too self-helpy on you is kind of the point of this book and, if you're afraid of that, go pick up a *Hustler* and really help yourself), but learning to love yourself is the greatest love of all, and it's a sign of really good taste, as long as you aren't gross.

P.S. You can disregard this entry if you are wearing white gloves because no matter what you're doing or what your taste is, you're far more sophisticated than we are.

How to Be Guiltless About Your Pleasures

The main thing that would make you feel guilty about your pleasures is other people and what they might think of you when they find out that you, for example, have every Celine Dion album on your iPod or watch Tyler Perry movies unironically (especially *For Colored Girls*). Fuck that noise right out of your head. Fuck your own face if that's what it takes. If something is good to you, it's good to you. You don't have to explain shit to anyone. Do you (in the face, again, if you must) and enjoy what you enjoy. Pleasure is pleasure, and it needs no modifiers to be qualified. High/low art debates are for babies.

The notion of a guilty pleasure suggests insecurity with your own sensibility. "I shouldn't like this thing that I do…" is nothing but a big old batch of cognitive dissonance. We understand what it is to feel this way, but we also understand what it is to grow the fuck up and stop being a baby about what other people think. If you feel guilty about some pleasures, you'll probably grow out of it. If you feel guilty about most pleasures, there is frankly something wrong with you. See a doctor.

As long as it doesn't make you guilty, you wimp, look to gay culture as a model for how to deal with the enjoyment of things that larger society feels are somehow lesser. Gay men and women have often already negotiated what it is to have desire outside of what is considered by idiots to be "normal." Furthermore, in the case of kitsch or camp or just enjoyable crappiness, the worst thing a person could be called for liking these things probably is "fag," and gay men have already been called that a lot. When there's no further threat for liking what you like, it's much easier to be open and okay with it.

The only time we can think of when one should truly feel guilty about pleasure is if that pleasure comes from hurting other people who don't want to be hurt. So all you serial killers out there should stop and think about what people would think of you. In this case, you really should feel guilty because you are. Of murder.

How to Be Sober

Reluctantly.

How to Be a Feminist

Not to be a buzz kill, but let's talk about feminism. The good news is that feminism isn't monolithic, so there are many ways to go about being a women's libber. It's kind of like Christianity in that it's based on one core belief (that women are people, too!), and yet there are a bajillion different subsets whose followers feel that the version they're practicing is superior to all others. And just like Christianity, it can be really preachy and boring.

So boring, in fact, we've been having a problem coming up with a way to talk about feminism and make it fun. But contrary to popular depictions of feminists as annoying harpies (Jesse Spano, Andrea Zuckerman, Lisa Simpson), real-life feminists have a real potential to be more fun than other girls because one set of beliefs within the movement is known as "sex-positive feminism," which initially began in response to anti-pornography feminists of old, but has evolved into what some call "raunch culture" or, in laymen's terms, "sluttiness." We love sluts. Who doesn't? We'll tell you who: "serious feminists." They are critical of what they call "fun feminism." Because for some feminists, fun is wrong.

Luckily, you don't have to listen to those feminists because there are so many others who'll gladly contradict them. If feminism were a test, it would be multiple choice. There's no one answer that's right for everyone, and there are so many subcategories in which you can find your niche. There are lipstick feminists, butch feminists, working-gal feminists, stay-at-home-mom feminists, leg-shaving feminists, armpit hair feminists, Dworkin feminists, Bright feminists, cat lady feminists, goldfish lady feminists, bisexual feminists, bilingual feminists, lesbian feminists, Lebanese feminists, rape feminists, funny feminists, humorless feminists, swinging feminists, sliding feminists, prudish feminists, rock 'n' roll feminists, R&B feminists, jazzy feminists, snazzy feminists, schnazzy feminists.

Even in the most extreme, didactic cases, all feminists mean well (if they really mean it), and we're all on the same team. In fact, our biggest error is when we forget that. Ultimately the worst thing one can do as a feminist is to tell another feminist how to be. So we're gonna stop right here.

How to Be Drama-Free

Wherever you are, plug your fingers in your ears and sing as loudly as possible (in the style of Mary J. Blige), "No. More. Drama! No. More. Drama!"

Oh wait, that probably seems pretty dramatic. Well, as experts (like Mary J. Blige) have proven and as we agree: this is too hard to answer.

Sorry!

How to Be on *Judge Judy*

Logistics (for Getting on Judge Judy, the Show)

- Bite off someone's finger.
- Cosign on a loan.
- Cash a check for someone you met on the Internet.
- Meet someone from the Internet.
- Turn a loan into a gift.
- Turn a gift into a loan.
- Steal your roommate's Tupperware.
- Kill an animal or let your animal kill an animal.
- Own a pit bull.
- Pour bleach on someone else's clothes.
- Hire tardy drivers for your limo company.
- Borrow someone's car.
- Do a ridiculous thing to someone else.
- Be a marginal person.
- Promise you'll pay someone back when you get your tax refund.
- Smoke pot and do anything.

Etiquette (for Dealing with Judge Judy, the Person)

- If you're a teenager and your lips are moving, she knows you're lying—best not to talk.
- Leave the baloney at the deli.
- It helps to know that 10 million people are watching you, but even if you don't, she'll remind you.
- Don't wear shorts or shirts that say, "BEER EQUALS FUN."
- Familiarize yourself with the expression, "Beauty fades, dumb is forever."

- You speak, she rules, and you shut up.
- There are no guarantees that she will not get mad; she's there *because* she gets mad.
- If she seems judgmental, it's because she is judging you. It's her job to call you a bad parent and/or an outrageous person.
- She can be any way she wants to be when someone's trying to pull the wool over her eyes.
- Don't tell her to listen.
- Don't ask how she's doing.
- Don't talk while she is talking.
- Don't pee on her leg and tell her it's raining.
- Flattery will get you nowhere.
- This is her playpen, not yours.
- "Um" is not an answer.
- Say "yes" instead of "yeah" on all references.
- Bring your listening ears.
- If you're going to lie, you have to have a good memory. And you don't. So don't lie.
- Make sure what you say is consistent with your prepared answer.
- You will not talk over her, so don't even try.
- God gave you two ears and one mouth for a reason—you're supposed to listen twice as much as you speak.
- Do not approach the bench—hand all photos and evidence to Bailiff Byrd.
- Don't say what they said—hearsay is not evidence. (She'll only accept letters from someone in active service.)
- Don't be afraid to call her "sir"—she's used to it (but you can tell she appreciates when people correct that mistake).
- On your best day, you aren't as smart as she is on her worst day when she's asleep.
- Judge Judy is always right.

How to Be All That You Can Be

Join the army.

How to Be Broke and Still Have Fun

Do you want to make more money? Of course. We all do. But that's not always possible overnight. In the meantime, you'll still want to get down and dance your troubles away or something. Just because you're poor doesn't mean life has to be boring. We've been there. We've *all* been there, except for Paris Hilton, although you could show your vagina to make some easy cash like Paris Hilton did. It could actually launch your career. But we don't recommend that. This is about having fun before you turn to porn and prostitution, although that could also be fun depending on your taste for penis, vagina, double penetration, condom blow jobs, and/or cameras.

Here are some tips that we found useful during our time in the trenches:

- Carry a flask when you go out at night. This will allow you to still get drunk without spending as much money. At crowded bars and clubs, you can order mixers for a fraction of the price of drinks and do it yourself. A warning, though: pulling this off in an empty space will expose your cheapness and also probably get you kicked out. Be smart and respectful about your sneakiness. Sneak easy. (See also, "How to Be Comfortable in a Club," page 56.)
- At Whole Foods, you'll find that the soup containers are opaque, priced by size, and much cheaper than the buffet food containers, which are transparent and typically priced according to weight. If you want an actual meal, instead of just warmed-up liquid, fill a soup container with the food of your choice from the buffet. You'll only be charged the soup price and you'll be eating the profits instead of slurping them.
- Go to a bar that serves free pizza with drinks and stock up.

- Get into video games to the point where you won't even want to leave the house, not even for food. This may run counter to actually finding work that will pull you out of relative poverty, but that's the trade-off for the good time that video games provide.
- If you're out of weed and don't have the funds to correct that situation, scrape your bowl for resin and then smoke that. You'll get at least high enough to forget that you just essentially checked the couch cushions of your smoking device for a quick hit.
- Find a shopping experience (such as Costco or a farmer's market) that specializes in pushing free samples. You can go around and make the free food into a meal. Literally, this is how Tracie ate lunch for years.
- Find outdoor concerts and stand outside of them.
- Locate a drive-in theater and strike up a friendship with a person who lives within viewing distance.
- Movie-hop. Buy one ticket and see four. Or however many you want. You're probably not working, so go crazy.
- If you can't afford a companion, go to the dog park and pet strange dogs. If it's the kind of dog park where you have to have a dog to enter, bring a leash and say your dog ran away and you thought maybe he came there and then pretend like you're distracted by all the other dogs. That will be time-consuming enough to make anyone stop caring about what you're doing.
- You'll notice that casino buses often show movies. Take in a film by driving alongside one and watching. This will only be economically feasible if you are going in the same direction as that bus anyway, but should you find yourself in this situation, you're in luck.
- Actually, if you aren't going to the casinos, you should. Go to Atlantic City, Las Vegas, or wherever and take advantage

of the free drinks, live bands, incredibly affordable buffets, and entertainment that is everywhere in the form of the wall-to-wall freaks. They are probably broke, too, so this is also a great opportunity to familiarize yourself with your people.

How to Be Cheered Up

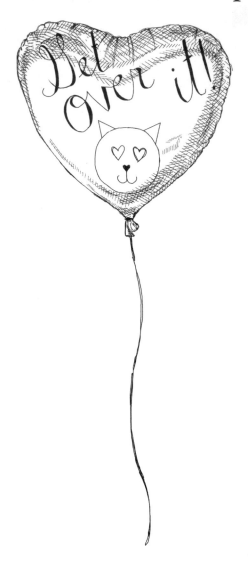

Look at this:

…and think about how lucky you are not to have grown up famous.

How to Be Happy

Don't worry.

How to Bee . . .

Name: Tracie Egan Morrissey and Rich Juzwiak

Title: Busy Buzzy Bee

Author: Karen Wallace

Circle one: Fiction   Nonfiction

Setting: (Where does the story take place?)

Busy Buzzy Bee takes place in a hive and outside of a hive and over a stream and past an oak tree and in a field and on a flower and a garden full of flowers. Depending on the point of view, you could also argue that it takes place on the bee because pollen, which is food for bees, is on the bee.

Character Names: Busy Bee, Queen Bee, drones, and grubs

Describe the main character. What kind of person is he or she?

First of all, she's not a person, she's a bee. Secondly, she's a really hard worker and selfless creature. She has the thankless job of collecting food and caring for other people's baby bees, which are so disgustingly ugly they might as well be actual babies. All the guys get to mate with the Queen while Busy Bee works until she dies. She doesn't die in the book, but you know it's coming.

The story begins with:

Busy Bee working. That is also how it ends.

The events in the story are: (include details)

Ugh, this book report is actual work. Fine.

1. After searching, Busy Bee finds a flower from which she collects nectar and pollen.
2. Once back at the hive, she dances to show her fellow workers how to find her flower nectar.

3. The worker bees make cells: some for honey, some for pollen, and some for the eggs that the queen bee lays.
4. Then Busy Bee goes around feeding everyone: first the drones (males), then the queen (bitch), and then the grubs (uglies).
5. After twelve days, the grubs change into bees through biology and weirdness. Busy Bee and the other worker bees touch the newborn bees with their feelers. If they were human, they'd be arrested for this.
6. With more mouths to feed, Busy Bee has to start all over to find another flower and get more pollen.
7. Busy Bee dies after an unsatisfying life (implied).

The story ends with:

Busy Bee and other bees dancing in a garden. This is probably all they can do to keep from killing themselves.

I learned that:

Female bees have it hard. They are the workers and responsible for everything.

I really liked:

When it was over.
Also, Busy Bee's indomitable spirit is infectious and hard not to admire, even though she is doomed from birth.

I didn't like when:

I saw the grubs, which look like maggots. Wet maggots. The photography in this reader for children of questionable intelligence is surprisingly crisp...to a fault.

I wonder:

What Busy Bee is doing right now. Oh no wait, we don't because we are sure she is working if not dead.

I would/would not recommend this book because:

We would because it's very informative, even though it's sad. It's at times painful to think about Busy Bee's hard life. It makes us not want to complain about things like getting to write books in air-conditioned apartments.

Busy Buzzy Bee is funny and fun. Especially when you learn (through the title) that bees are both busy and buzzy.

How to Be . . .

Wow, are you still reading? You aren't tired yet? Maybe you should smoke more.

As you know from reading, you've certainly come to the right place if you're curious about how to be. If you've read this book, you should have a good idea already. This is to say, we advocate being a good reader just as much as we don't endorse bestiality. Those two things are at the opposite ends of our endorsement continuum. If you're a good enough reader, you probably don't have time to have sex with anything, let alone animals. We don't advocate reading in the place of sex, unless what you want to have sex with walks on four legs or has a pouch.

We'd also probably advocate that a good way to be is unconcerned with the opinions of people on dope—were we not on dope ourselves. Too bad, that's what we all signed up for.

Really, our list of core principles when it comes to you solving your problems is simple:

1. See a doctor.
2. Think about what Judge Judy would do.
3. In the case of heartache, consult Mariah Carey's catalog. Start with "Breakdown" and work your way out.
4. Always be honest.
5. Except in those instances where being honest would be rude.
6. It's important to strike a balance between having manners and being true to yourself. Don't pay compliments that you don't mean and don't say "Excuse me" if you don't want to be excused. Think, really think.
7. A good way to be is not so concerned with what other people think of you, unless those other people have written a book. We are the ones who rule the world through judgment. That said, the best way to be is be yourself.*

*Clarification: Yourself as filtered through us.

Outro: Thank-yous and Shoutouts

First of all, we have to give a big thank-you to the person who invented the phrase "thank you." Without you, this page would not be possible.

Second of all, thank you to our parents, who understand the value of an education because they picked up the tab for ours.

Thanks to our other family members for being polite enough to refrain from judging us to our faces.

Thanks to Dan Morrissey and Cory Soulette for having to suffer through a year's worth of stupid conversations about a book in which we give really stupid advice. You two are the wind beneath our wings.

Thank you to our editor, Emily Griffin, who helped with support and advice every step of the way, and who took every single question of ours seriously, including, "What's your stance on depicting animal boners?" and "Can we put a human breast on the cover of our book?"

Thanks to Daniel Greenberg and Monika Verma at the Levine Greenberg Agency, as well as Jezebel's founding editor, Anna Holmes, for whipping our asses into shape and believing in our ability to turn something so ludicrous into a book. You did it, guys!

Thanks to our holy trinity of Judge Judy, Anna Nicole Smith, and Mariah Carey for being sources of both entertainment and enlightenment. Mariah, thanks especially for "Breakdown" and "We Belong

Together." Oh, and the "Fantasy" remix with Ol' Dirty Bastard is also classic.

Thank you to blueberries for existing and keeping Rich fed and full of antioxidants.

Thank you to Sabra for making the best store-bought hummus in existence. Thanks to the people who make that vegetarian chicken salad we got at the deli that we don't remember the brand name of.

Thank you for being a friend, *Golden Girls*.

Thank you to our pets for being good distractions from hard work. And thanks for being shitty distractions, as well, sometimes literally.

Thanks in advance to our friends on the Internet and in media who we'll be calling upon for help in getting the word out on this book. You guys are killing it!

Thanks to Tyra Banks for being a monster and always giving us something to laugh at.

Thanks to Big and Little Edie Beale for having lived and loved staunchly.

Thanks to puppets for being weird and scary.

Thanks to all of the children in beauty pageants and the parents who pushed them there. You have truly fulfilled your goal of entertaining, even if it's not the way you intended.

Thank you to Whitney Houston. We will always love you. And we always did, even in the *Being Bobby Brown* years. Actually, especially in the *Being Bobby Brown* years.

Thank you to *Saw* for providing the opportunity to say, on a yearly basis, "Are we going to see *Saw* this weekend?" See *Saw*, get it? What a ride it's been!

Thank you to the religious zealots for giving us something to ponder.

Thank you to the strippers who keep reality TV interesting and well-heeled in Lucite.

Thank you to Jean. Your letter was the best we ever got.

Thank you to anybody weird, really. We enjoy ya.

Thank you to anyone who could be considered "special" or "exceptional." You truly are God's children.

Thanks to EZ Wider rolling papers, because short of eating pot, we always got the highest with your help (even though Tracie swears by bongs, whatever).